Life Organizer

◆

Personal Magick

Life Organizer

◆

Personal Magick

Joel B. Brown

Garden Tree Fountains Press

Life Organizer – Personal Magick

Copyright 2013 by Joel B. Brown

ISBN: 978-0-615-90952-3

Library of Congress Control Number: 2013953444

Printed in the United States of America.

All rights reserved. No part of this book may be used or reproduced in any manner whatsoever without written permission, except the three blank forms, which are provided for the reader.

Book & cover design, prepress services:
Kate Weisel, Bellingham, WA (weiselcreative.com)

Cover image: Eye of Providence, ©Igor Zakowski
use rights purchased from Fotolia.com

A previous version was published in 1979 as *Life Organizer*
by American Information Distributors.

For information please visit the web site

gardentreefountains.com

This work is dedicated to my grandsons,
Bryce Manibusan and Stefan Swanson,
and all those who wish they could fly.

Acknowledgment

My special thanks to those who have encouraged and assisted in the production of this book: My wife Rose, Dr. Edward Sullivan, Linda Rahman, Nancy Hathaway, Calvin Brown, Monica Swanson, Joshua Tenorio, and Kate Weisel.

Contents

Acknowledgment. vii

Preface 1
    The Name. 1
    The Purpose 3
    Universe. 3
    Tree of Life 4
    Genesis 5
        Alternate Spellings 6

Introduction. 9
    General Purpose 9
    Theory Sources. 9
    A Few Postulates to Get Us Going 10
    Observational Learning 11
    Techniques Presented 12
    Paradigm of the ***Life Organizer – Personal Magick***. 13
    Getting Started with Theory 14
        Chapter One – Preview –
        Subjects Related to your State of Mind. 14
        Chapter Two – Preview –
        Subjects Related to Natural Mechanism of Mind 15
        Chapter Three – Preview – Change Management 16

Chapter One – Subjects Related to Your State of Mind 17

How the following sections should affect you 17
    Being Your Pragmatic Self 17
    Effectiveness 21
    Balance 21
    Different Types of Thoughts. 23
    Images. 25
    Mindset 27
    The Astral Hologram 28
    Dividing the Whole – Meta View 29
    Cardinal Directions. 30
    Pre-wave Broadcast 31
    Fact and Truth 33
    Faith 33
    Secrets 35
    Opportunities. 36
    Return on Investment 36
    Zen of Making a Choice 38
    What to Leave In, What to Take Out 40
    Pre-plan Your Return Trip 40
    How to Get What You Want 41
    Manage your Plan of Attack 43

Chapter Two – Subjects Related to Natural Mechanisms of Mind . . 47

    Meditation Ritual. 48
    Cleansing and Protecting Space 53
    Raising Consciousness 54
    Ask and You Shall Receive! 55
    Quotations from the King James Bible: 56

Chapter Three – Change Management 61
Moving Forward 61
The Analysis. 62
Flaws to Ceremony Chart 63
Script Templates 65
Technique to Install a Program into Your Unconsciousness 67
Technique to Request Guidance from
    Your Holy Guardian Angel 69
Technique to Plant a Seed in the Womb of Nature
    via Universal Mind 72
Identify Flaws. 75
    Example – Flaws Form 75
Set Processes 76
    Looking at the example Flaws Form 77
    Example – Processes Form 77

Chapter Four – Mystical Glossary 79
Some Generic Trap Names 80
    Example #1 – Traps Form 81
About Reading a Dictionary 83
    Example #2 – Traps Form 85

Bibliography. 87
Appendix A – Metaphysical Notes 89
Development from Naught 90
Appendix B – Tree of Life Symbol 91
Appendix C – Forms 93
Flaws Form. 93
Processes Form 94
Traps Form 95
About Author 97
Alone 99

Preface

This book is intended for those who would like to improve themselves in a spiritual way. I remember years ago how I was unsure about studying the mystical path, let alone involvement in a belief system of religion. It took years for me to plunge fully into the subject of this book. I want to give some assurance to others entering into the mystical that in fact it is a valid way to enlighten your soul and add value to your life in general. By doing so, we also achieve the overarching goal of presenting a good and improved examples to others.

However, it takes a lifetime to get a good understanding of the entire subject. So, I have chosen to present a specific area of the occult that will be of practical value in polishing the soul, getting on the path of wisdom, and gaining a feeling of unbound, fearless optimism toward the task.

The Name

You might wonder why the title **Life Organizer – Personal Magick**. "Life" has to do with consciousness. "Organizer" has to do with taking parts of the whole, grouping together certain functional parts and using them as functional organs in a network. In **Life Organizer – Personal Magick** paradigm, I use groupings of mental/spiritual conceptions as virtual organic functions, which have the ability to affect the physical world.

The method is to create a program for your unconscious to execute, appeal to your Holy Guardian Angel[1] or interact with the Universal Grand Mind. These program units can be tied to one another so that each program might work as a virtual organ within a virtual network.

The concept of a virtual organic network is really not so new. As we all know there is the physical body (a network of physical organs.) We find the neural network with its electro-chemical communications. We find the endocrine system of messaging using receptors on specific cells. On

---

1 Here is a definition from <u>Abrahadabra</u> by Rodney Orpheus: "The Holy Guardian Angel is an angel that is unique to each person – a special spiritual entity that guides and guards you."

a more subtle level we have interpretation of pressure waves: hearing, Vascular Autonomic Signal (VAS)[2] and so on. On a finer level there is the informational recognition of vibrations passed along by electric current and electro-magnetic fields.[3]

A subtler level of human interpretation is recognizing a failed attempt, which causes one to say to oneself "I'll never do that again based on memory of this experience." The methods in the **Life Organizer – Personal Magick** are an intelligent enhancement of our inherent ability to build upon our own natural facilities.

I am not saying that such a virtual organ is like a part of our physical body such as the cerebellum or the heart. Nor am I saying that an organ of the mind might become encoded into DNA such that a physical organ could develop.

However I might suggest that such a virtual organ be used to adjust the production of chemicals in the body. For example, I might set up a program based on certain triggers that induce a sudden surprise or the opposite, a sudden relaxation. In this a case the program initiation would trigger the sympathetic or parasympathetic response through the ensuing emotion and resultant flow of hormones.

I sub-title **Life Organizer** with **Personal Magick** because in the true sense of the definition, magick is:

- "The Science and Art of causing Change in accordance with the Will." – Aleister Crowley

- "High Magick is the transformation of the Self to the Higher Self." – Llewellyn, publisher.

This book is all about self-improvement by self-programming or reaching out to your Holy Guardian Angel and the Grand Mind for help and direction and using the Mystical Glossary. As you improve yourself you will be better able to make changes according to your will. This is just one of many types of magick but a very effective and personal one.

---

2 <u>Ariculotheropy Manuall</u> 2nd Edition by Terry Oleson Ph.D.
3 <u>The Secret Teachings of Plants</u> by Stephen Harrod Buhner.

The Purpose

Beyond showing others a good example, what we get from life are discrete understandings based on our soul's accumulation of experiences, insights about our relations with over souls and the spiritual network or hierarchy.

Not everyone is expected to fathom the understandings of someone else totally, and there is no important reason for you to grasp all of what I say in the theory presented, in particular, the cosmology of the One (*One is generally referred to as God – in the context of this book Ones are equated to the continuous production of God's development in the expanding universe*) and the parity between the Ones and how Archetypes[4] are involved with the Ones. If you can acquire any information that leads you to better understanding about the world, that is good for the soul.

This book includes both basic practical methods and advanced theory intending to support the practical claims made. If you are not familiar with reading occult text, it might take multiple reads and research into other books to become comfortable.

Universe

When I refer to Universe I am addressing a single living whole with the given name of Universe. It will be more appropriate to refer to Cosmos when referring to the inherent workings of the universal machine. Cosmos is the workings of energy and information within Universe. This is a shift of perspective from a dead universe to a single living universal organism, and every contained object or entity within it is a moving/changing part of Cosmos.

---

4   Archetype refers to the first occurrence of a pattern, similar to the meaning of a prototype when referring to an object. The Archetype name is referred to whenever the pattern occurrences are noticed.

Tree of Life

This is a living metaphor — a symbol of how energy is transformed from the ultimate source into the entire universe. The Tree of Life[5] is used in ancient and current Jewish Qabalah. You will find a diagram of the Tree and the worlds described by the Tree in Appendix B.

To understand the Tree of Life is to understand the archetypal[6] ways energy is transformed on the finest levels. In the Tree of Life symbology, all the world's mythologies can be seen played out using Anthropomorphism, or bringing to life (animation), universal forces which endlessly repeat themselves. In this book I utilize an archetype which literally defines the world of Briah, but whose operations create effects on all spheres in all worlds.

The universal process within the sphere of Kether (source of all Emanations), whereby Self-realization (of God) is repeatedly expressed as "One" (the precursor to physical reality), produces alternating potential differences in polarity; it is this quality of "Ones" that allows adhesion of "Ones" to each other and to be counted in the physical kingdom. This potential polarity is the underlying structure of what I refer to as one of the universal mechanisms of Mind. This particular mechanism is an Archetype which I refer to as "Archetype of Reflection" because it operates by division and multiplication of two.

The Spiritual Logos (of God's self-realization) pervades all worlds from top to bottom, allowing the Mechanisms of Universal Mind to pervade all levels as well. The world of the Archetypal of Reflection, called Briah (Creation), is humanly impenetrable, having a surface appearing as a refraction of Kether's process, the Source. Inside the dim view of Kether reveals the dynamics which affect the next world down called Yetzirah (Formative).

A question presented to Briah, via your Holy Guardian Angel reflected back is processed through the spheres of Yetzirah to the inquirer in Assiyah (Kingdom, made physical) with the answer embedded.

---

5   See Tree of Life diagram in Appendix B.
6   Like a prototype of a mechanical procedure or object, an archetype comes into existence upon the first example in Universe.

Although we say "unknowable" in reference to worlds above Yetzirah, or indeed above Assiyah (the physical world), and though our five senses cannot detect those worlds, we can have a dim vision of how the next world down is affected by the world above it. The world of Briah (of Creation) resonates and passes the resonation energy downward through the veil *(what I call the mirrored surface)* into lower worlds — "as above so below."[7] Spirit contains the capacity to pass images of **symbolic information or questions of something unknowable** to both the unconscious and the conscious mind. It is this mechanism that shines through into lower worlds (Yetzirah and Assiyah). By the very nature of the spheres in Yetzirah your special request is resolved by processing the image you presented to Briah via your Holy Guardian Angel and finally reflects into the reality of Assiyah (Grounding by completing the circle.)

Genesis

The first page of the Christian Bible speaks of the Genesis of Universe, which science refers to as the Big Bang. Although I think there are some missing parts in the Big Bang theory, it will work as a metaphor. Among the seemingly contentious concepts of Genesis, i.e., Big Bang and Trinity, I have resolved to my satisfaction a workable unified concept of a Supreme Consciousness, Spirit, God, and Totality of all Self-Realization in Universe.

To analyze the Big Bang we can proceed conceptually with mathematics. Energy is going to be released from a potential or allowed to exist. The potential to produce a "One" is contained within the Naught of Universe. That means from no-thing, no God, there is a potential to produce a universe. **Naught produces a "One" when Self-Realization occurs from the potential.** This means that one occurrence of a Naught becoming self-aware produces a One.

---

[7] (See: The Unwritten Qabalah, chapter 4 of <u>The Mystical Qabalah</u> by Dion Fortune; Chapter "One", section "Before His Throne...", page 56 <u>Sefer Yetzirah</u>, by Aryeh Kaplan; and, Chapter "Divinity", <u>A Kabbalistic Universe</u>, by Z'ev ben Shimon Halevi).

Collective Consciousness must be everyone's consciousness combined and the details of all associated awareness. The collective (Grand) Mind must be the set of tools which can be utilized to access Collective Consciousness.

In the theory of Qabalah, in its simplest form, there are four somewhat overlapping worlds:[8]

Alternate Spellings[9]

Root	Emanations	Azilut	Atziluth
Trunk	Creation	Beriah	Briah
Branch	Formation	Yezirah	Yetzirah
Fruit	Making	Asiyyah	Assiyah

The metaphysical is connected to the physical through sentient life force. Humans, for example, are metaphysical by virtue of their consciousness, which can choose to affect physical material with the body.

The discipline of physics has led to finding "objects" or magnet fields much smaller than the electron and it seems that the deeper we look we find a layer of smaller forms. From the Qabalistic Tree of Life metaphysical theory, each Tree is only a sphere of a larger Tree and that pattern continues; every sphere within a tree harbors a smaller, yet complete Tree of Life symbol.

When a repeating pattern appears on all levels, such as the perspective size of the Tree of Life, the increasingly smaller objects or small wave riding on a larger wave, it is a phenomena that proves itself to be foundational within Universe. Its discovery means a deep truth has been found.[10]

In the primordial Universe, at the very beginning, there are no such numbers as two, three, four, et cetera, because Naught only produces a "One"

---

8   See Tree of Life in Appendix B.
9   The names of the worlds and of the sephiroth are spelled in various ways, depending on the reference.
10 There is a similar pattern described in Chapter IX in <u>An Elementary Textbook of Psychoanalysis</u>, by Charles Brenner, MD, as found in myths, religions, or cultures.

in Atziluth. Only Two is active in Briah. Three and greater numbers are active in Yetzirah and Assiyah.

Each time Naught in Atziluth produces a discrete "One", there is exactly the same, undifferentiated accumulation of Self-Realization that is an expression of consciousness. There is an increasing number of individual Ones, downstream to become matter in the world Assiyah, and an accumulation of the same Self, so that God is the single conceptual assimilation of Self that is spread over the entire sea of Ones. God, therefore, is in all lower worlds, exists as Self in all developments of counting two and higher, in the form of over souls and individual souls, and of all other configurations of "Ones". The Big Bang is still in action – we call it the expansion of the universe, the expression of all possibilities. The cutting edge formulating all possibilities can be seen in the life of stars and creation of babies – and all other change.

This production of "Ones" occurs in Atziluth. The next world downstream, Briah, is produced by attributes from the potential within Naught, inherited by and passed on to One during Self Realization. The Archetype of Reflection is dormant in Naught, but is a potential in Self-realization of One. Self-Realization requires two potentials of reflection to produce the One. This is where "God" sees Its reflection against the sea of Naught and that reflection results in Self-realization once. It is the production of the attribute of polarity which is passed on as a potential within the "One".

What initiated the Big Bang? I have found that I don't need much time to speculate on this. I easily find two possibilities, either of which I am okay with.

- Naught is a Universal Spore.
- Naught is a Universal Node through which this universe is pouring forth from a stream of Universes.

In other words, the first Point would be either similar to a spore that grows into a universe or else Universe is currently passing through a Node from some other unknown source. Or maybe the One and only God should be defined as this unknown source – it does not matter to this book. What I needed was a complete concept to link the source of both physics and metaphysics.

This Archetype of Reflection would be the prime initiator in aligning polar energy based on the potential within each "One". One way of imagining the production of "Ones" is like this:

> In the conceptual center of Naught there is what looks like a spinning token, which is one side black and one side white. The token alternates from black to white at the exact instant of Self-realization, and with that is the "One" produced. At this point normalcy is the side of white, so when the token spins to the black side more Self-realization and another "One" is produced with a black polarity. And so on.

Here is another way to explain the metaphysical phenomenon:

> Exercising the potential to acknowledge Naught is to manifest a "One". Acknowledgement unlocks what was dormant so that the dormant becomes active, which then is aware of its birth, as well as the concept of mother, father and son; Trinity in potential in the emanation level of Atziluth, polarity on the Creative level of Briah, Formations on the level of Yetzirah, and Manifestation on the level of Assiyah.

The potential of manifestation[11] lies in the concept of Naught. Immediately upon the first realization there is Consciousness. Consciousness was the realization of itself, that it was the reflection of Nothing. The Consciousness was and is the realization that It was opposite of Nothing. To be aware of Self was to acknowledge the opposite so as to become Nothing and immediately spawn another "One", but of the opposite polarity potential. Now there were two of the same but they cannot be the same – the difference between the two "Ones" was the going back to Nothing or Death. The "Ones" alternate the display of one pole, then the other.

The "Ones" pour into the world of Briah and begins the division of "Ones" between positive and negative. So the Archetype of Reflection was born after the first "One" was born and it defines the world of Briah.

---

11 See The Mystical Qabalah, by Dion Fortune.

Introduction

General Purpose

1. To provide techniques by which one can develop and improve existing abilities and meet the underlying, compelling moral obligation to show a better example to others.

2. To present a reasonable theory to understand Universe,[12] and Cosmos, and the division between matter and mind – the physical and the metaphysical.

3. To provide a format by which one might analyze his or her current ineptitudes, flaws and liabilities, which if refined, would improve his or her example to others.

Theory Sources

In the search for wisdom and understanding by studying Qabalah, Tree of Life, Christianity, Zen, Tao, physics, metaphysics, and mathematics, common beliefs and opinions violate the foundational policies of balance and neutrality, such as for example, Zen's 'Beginners Mind' or Jesus's 'Becoming Childlike'.

Some beliefs and opinions are acceptable because they temporarily bridge a gap in resources. However, acceptance may carry a heavy burden if that belief or opinion continues beyond its immediate use. We are bridled by such insidious processes going on in our minds. These beliefs and opinions can be found out and put to rest. This is one of the primary reasons for this book.

I have referenced books that I encourage you to read, although a complete theoretical understanding is not really necessary to get started.

---

12 As it is somewhat difficult to find a clear understanding of Cosmos versus Universe I will give you my understanding from Oxford English definition of each: Universe is the entire collection of the manifested world. Cosmos is the entire Universe as an integrated working whole; it still is all of Universe but includes information and intelligence.

A Few Postulates to Get Us Going

- ❖ Each person has a unique set of issues, with individual ways of solving them. For many people, regression and denial are the default.

- ❖ Everyone does their best in life according to their available personal resources.

- ❖ People mostly learn by observing others.

- ❖ Everyone has a moral obligation to show the best example possible and to improve one's self to be a better example in the future. It is further valuable to pass this process along to others whenever and wherever possible.

- ❖ Everyone has the power to affect positive changes in their world that will be reflected in Universe at large.

- ❖ *You and everyone can and should make a major difference!*

Observational Learning

It is easy enough to discover firsthand how dynamically babies and older children learn from those around them.[13] As we observe Nature, we become creative by copying processes already in existence.

> *Main article: <u>Observational learning</u>*
> The learning process most characteristic of humans is imitation; "One's personal <u>repetition</u> of an <u>observed</u> behavior, such as a <u>dance</u>. Recent research [*citation needed*] with children has shown that observational learning is well suited to seeding behaviors that can spread widely across a culture through a process called a diffusion chain, where individuals initially learn a behavior by observing another individual perform that behavior, and then serve as a model from which other individuals learn the behavior. **Humans can copy three types of information simultaneously: the demonstrator's goals, actions, and environmental outcomes** (results, see Emulation, observational learning). Through copying these types of information, (most) infants will tune into their surrounding culture. Humans aren't the only creatures capable of learning through observing. A wide variety of species learn by observing. In "One" study, for example, pigeons watched other pigeons set reinforced for either pecking at the feeder or stepping on a bar. When placed in the box later, the pigeons tended to use whatever technique they had observed other pigeons using earlier. (Zentall, Sutton & Sherburne, 1996) [*full citation needed*].
> Observational learning involves a neural component as well. Mirror neurons, then, may play a critical role in the imitation of behavior as well as the prediction of future behavior. (Rizzolatti, 2004) [*full citation needed*]. Mirror neurons are thought to be represented in specific sub regions in the frontal and parietal lobes, and there is evidence that individual sub regions respond most strongly to observing certain kinds of actions
>
> ~ Extract taken from wikipedia.com

---

13 Additional discussion of this can be found on page 5, <u>Biofeedback</u>, third edition, by M. Schwartz and F. Amdrasik.

From the first paragraph in the extract (*see bold sentence*):

> "Humans can copy three types of information simultaneously: the demonstrator's goals, actions, and environmental outcomes."

So, using the techniques in this book will allow others to see you in a better form but they will learn to improve themselves too.

We, therefore, have an imperative moral obligation to show our best example, to improve ourselves so as to show a better example, and thus to improve the whole of mankind, moment by moment in a purposeful, cooperative and deliberate way.

Techniques Presented

- Raising your conscious to a higher spiritual plane
- Accessing Universal Mind[14] (via the Mystical Glossary).

    Entering and initiating a Trap entry into Mystical Glossary, e.g., an obstacle resolution, questions, or requests for direction with respect to your purpose, will intrinsically initiate communication between you and the upper worlds via Universal Grand Mind.

- Creating a program and a script (much like an hypnosis script) for its installation into your unconscious mind, with the ability to initiate program execution.

    When a program becomes part of your unconsciousness, it will be executed with triggers and specified parameters inherent in the program description or provided by the installation script.

- Appealing to your Holy Guardian Angel

    This technique is useful when aspiring for guidance, wisdom or a tree of knowledge.

---

14 Processes occurring within Universe and can be seen in the Tree of Life spheres. Universal Mind can be accessed as described in this book.

- Planting a seed in the Womb of Nature

    When you plant a seed using the Mechanism of Mind, a tree of knowledge is conceived and will grow and become available to you. Access will happen by asking your Holy Guardian Angel or the information will appear in your mind at appropriate times.

Paradigm of the *Life Organizer – Personal Magick*

The **Life Organizer – Personal Magick** utilizes similar but more sophisticated techniques and mechanisms of the original Life Organizer but approaches self-improvement from a different angle.

Whereas the original **Life Organizer** was designed for the aspirant to set anything as goals including ordinary wants and desires, this edition has been designed to identify, first of all, your personal problems and flaws (*inadequacies, useless opinions, improper values, weaknesses, talent omissions in education and training, and so on*) preventing you from displaying a good[15] or improved example to others.

You don't necessarily need to understand all of the concepts and theories at first; **you do need to be sincere about progressing toward self improvement — of showing a better example to others**. Understanding will come with practice; in fact, you might use Chapter Four – Mystical Glossary to ask for greater understanding about subjects presented in this book. (See Example #1 – Trap: *Advanced Studies, Order of Knowledge*.)

---

15 Good is subjective, of course. I would like to mention that perfection is not always a good thing either. Anal retention or obsessive compulsive may seem good to some people but they lack balance and practicality.

Getting Started with Theory

Chapter One – Preview – Subjects Related to your State of Mind

This chapter is all about you but little to do with your physical body. In order to communicate with the world at large (Universe), you may need to adjust your conscious attitude. The following are some areas of your attitude which may need to be refined to maintain balance and to set your mood when attempting self-improvement:

- Having respect for all things at all times.

- Learning self-abandon[16] – a place of no self-pity (See Personal Space in Chapter Two.).

- Being remorsefully unencumbered – to quit feeling guilty over past events

- Sobriety – eliminating cynicism, uncontrollable sexual desires, manifestations of greed, materialism, self-importance, vanity and petty wants.

- Asserting unbending intent in doing what is right for mankind.

- Confidence built on a solid foundation of formula over trial and error (where formulas were discovered originally by trial and error).

- Heightened awareness of your own components and spiritual connection.

- The impeccability of always following through and not giving in to the easy way over the right way.

- Inner silence or meta-observation of the ego's stubbornness, arrogance, narrow mindedness, conceit, and egotistical self-talk that is really a plagiarism of outside thoughts entering your mind.

---

16 Self-abandon is giving up the belief and supporting reasons of your ego that you are special. A term used extensively by don Jaun of Carlos Castaneda.

- Accepting the truth of your certain spiritual achievement, and honoring yourself and Universe of which you are a very important part.

This list is surely formidable for the neophyte; however, when you read through these chapters you will begin to feel the importance of your role in Universe and what you are really doing for yourself and others. When the importance is truly seen you will find it much easier to subscribe to the new mood that will make your goals attainable.

What makes change seem difficult is your uncertainty about doing something you have not done before – there is always hesitance, a smack of doubt. After following properly laid out procedures a few of times, confidence will prevail, and you will bypass this doubt, making the process easier.

To be in the proper mood for communication with Universal Mind or your Holy Guardian Angel is not a matter of perfecting all items above, rather this list is intended to reveal aspects of your state of mind requiring sobriety and sincerity. Chapter One will help prepare this state of mind. In Chapter Two, I discuss creating your personal space or "place-of-no-pity"[17] (*a space on the astral plane – the sphere of Yesod*). It will assist automatically in the task of setting the mood.

Chapter Two – Preview –
Subjects Related to Natural Mechanism of Mind

This Chapter is about Universe (macrocosm), all that is not your personal world (microcosm). Imagine you are in your private place-of-no-pity surrounded by your micro-cosmic world. There are several Universal Mechanisms you can employ to communicate outside of your personal world. This is not communicating in the normal sense; you present a dialogue along with images as you speak to the appropriate entity – Holy Guardian Angel, Grand Mind or the unconscious part of your mind; then wait for the corresponding answers in the form of changed reality.

---

17 The Power of Silence, by Carlos Castaneda.

Chapter Three – Preview – Change Management

This is the chapter where you will analyze yourself, plan the changes you would like to make, and finally communicate those changes to your unconsciousness, your Holy Guardian Angel or the Universal Mind via mechanisms and techniques explained in Chapter Two.

Chapter One – Subjects Related to Your State of Mind

This chapter is intended to put you in a state of mind conducive to allowing communication between you and the macrocosm using mechanisms of Universe.

The sections below contain subjects that should be considered for the purposes of effectiveness and efficiency and to help define a new mind set. In this chapter I present ideas without proof and do not solicit your sanction, unless you are intellectually inclined to agree. However, I have used all of the techniques presented many years with excellent results.

In order to prepare your new personal mindset properly you certainly want to leave behind all useless, if not detrimental, opinions and habits.

Here is how the following sections should affect you:

During the reading of **Being Your Pragmatic Self,** I expect you will relax your personal views and adjust your perspective. In other words, relax the artificial values you give to physical objects and cultural conveniences, the values taught to you from babyhood.

Being Your Pragmatic Self

People in general are so wrapped up in drama and other emotions that they forget or perhaps never recognize their organic relationships to the inorganic. Changing the locality of your focus can put you into a more pragmatic mood and thus modify your perspective.

In your mind you are able to see (or accept) the material items around you as energy fields, which have attributes projected from their core.

When I say "core" I do not mean a single thing like a center of gravity, but rather an inner layer like the sphere[18] of Yesod, in the world of Yetzirah overlapping the sphere of Malkuth in the world of Assiyah.

As humans we have to participate, as needed, in the physical world, but we must unceasingly be aware and cautious with the metaphysical. Being pragmatic is not intended to anticipate what the Great Unknown will bring. Rather, pragmatic means we need to plan our world development as best we can in harmony with Nature. This is a tribute to the fact that everything changes constantly – both physically and metaphysically!

The core of an entity projects into a lower sphere and so displays an energy field; this being so, spiritual entities form their living bodies by assimilating dust from the thin layer of usable, organic material covering Earth. Let me give you a visual:

> *Think of a sponge touching the surface of water. If you focus closely in your mind you will see the water moving in various directions to collect in all parts of the sponge (capillary action). Now think about a complex electro-magnetic field nearing the surface of a dust covered earth. Again if you let your imagination focus closely you would certainly see charged dust moving in various directions to collect in all parts of the field.*

In both animate and inanimate entities there are cores, which emanate and command different sets of attributes. Some universal energetic entities are given names, which we see written into classical mythology. This is the meaning of **Anthropomorphism** – the way of looking at repeating energetic patterns, such as we see in the playing out of Oedipus, respect for your father, respect for your boss, respect for your social leader, and leader of your religion, and awe for the Grand Mind. In fact, the symbol of the Tree of Life is so complete that all parts of the cosmos can be placed in an appropriate sphere or on a path between the spheres.

There is a particular archetype[19] that can be seen in what is known as

---

18   Please refer to Appendix B for a brief discussion of the Worlds and Spheres of the Tree of Life.
19   The Anthropomorphized name of the first occurrence of a repeating pattern.

Complementarity.[20] It works on the level of the pre-primordial. It is active in setting up the potential of polarity – think spinning disk where the axis penetrates the disk from one edge to the opposite edge, where only one side of a coin can be seen at a time. You can see it in the study of quantum physics; where light can be either a wave or particle. Both are valid but you can only detect one at a time, think paradox. In the case, where metaphysics meets physics, is where we can recognize complementarity.

In terms of our connections to the rest of nature, the nervous system participates electrically in receiving and transmitting via its electro-magnetic fields, which extends out from the body. Each person is a communication node. Of course we are much more than that but this definition attributes the basic qualities of all living organisms.

In a mundane sense, the body's function is to transform your will into action – meta-physical control of physical movement in the three dimensional realm. During transformation, energy fields appear to us as changing reality, carrying the format and complexion of our thoughts. We can engage tools of change to the surface of energy fields to affect them, allowing alterations which match our conscious thinking. Coupled with the ability to change the physical world are the abilities of sensing light with the eyes, sound with the ears, texture with tactile feeling, taste with the tongue, and smell with the nose.

There is another method of altering the physical world. It is really a link between you and another person, that is, with voice vibrations. The power of the voice is metaphysical and affects physical change.

What we sometimes think of as reality is only the physical part, even though most of that is of no use for the life of an organism other than construction; only a thin layer of dust-like material on earth can be used by living creatures except for structures built of calcium for security and mobility.

Organisms are not made of much physical matter, but if you look with a meta-view of the expanding universe, you will see that procreation of life is at the cutting edge of the expanding universe. The non-physical is

---

20 See <u>The Black Hole War</u>, by Leonard Susskind.

where we see so much variation, permutations and possibilities.

Health will allow you to enjoy many physical privileges and since the body is a part of the physical world and a projection from within, its description is subject to "thoughtful" change. However, since you cannot erase your personal history, changing your physical body is more difficult than changing your mind set and attitude. Physical change depends on what you consume, your exercise, mental wellbeing, and seeing yourself as being in a state of health.

Always picture your physical body and mind as you would most like to be; eating proper foods, getting good exercise, and keeping clean and aesthetically pleasing. Visualize yourself running miles at a time, dancing exquisitely; swimming great distances and doing all the other actions you admire (projecting yourself in 'Your World' all these ways). Changing your mind set within will cause a new projection onto your world's energy surface. Returning home after a weeklong trip and escaping the normal energy patterns that you are commonly around, will give you an idea of how a change in mental attitude and mindset can allow the physical world to be more plastic, enjoyable, relaxing and effective. Reality is dependent on the situation you are in.

Once you learn that your body moves as a result of your own imaginations you will find it easier to accept that the rest of your environment will change also as a result of your personal imaginations. Remember your environment is to a large extent your personal world projection.

The "I", which we all know so intimately, includes all spirited creatures. It includes organic and inorganic creatures that can be invoked or evoked.[21] Given the right conditions there are hardly any limits to your development.

---

[21] Invocation refers to bringing within you; evocation refers to bringing inside your world, but outside of, you.
Invocation is the mental act of bringing inside your world an entity or image capable of initiating processes.
Evocation is similar except the entity is kept outside your world. This is a particular case where the protective circle and banishment are used for special protection. You would not invoke an evil spirit but you might evoke that spirit with special precautions. You might invoke a god of good reputation to assist with good deeds. In either case you would be frugal to specify particular spiritual attributes when defining what can enter your world.

Generally what gives us grief is wanting. The cause of our wanting is ignorance, lack of a good role model, and misinformation. In your pragmatic mindset the importance of wanting over needing should be diminished because wanting simply causes a false sense of needing and creates unnecessary, if not deleterious, karma. I hope this section has helped bring your thinking into a down-to-earth perspective.

Effectiveness

Each time you make a movement, the easier it is to do such movement precisely. The same is true with thinking. It may be difficult at first to make break or replace a habit, but it soon can become rote.

When you follow through with stated plans, you increase the probability of successful achievements for your plans in the future. The longer you focus on your improvement plans, the more it will map out your veritable future and the more clear your thinking will become. In a situation where you are about to construct something, visualizing a complete image always precedes effective construction. Thus, to be successful in building, it is vital to see all of the parts fitting together holistically.

The thoughts you have will change the world around you. When you are certain of what you need, as with a vacuum, it will be drawn to you. See your goal in your mind and the process by which it will become yours. Conversely, if you want NOT to have something happen then clearly see in your mind how it will be prevented.

Balance

There is no perfect balance in either the physical or metaphysical; there are just too many physical influences and too many symbolic and psychic influences in the meta-physical. Balance, in this context, is meant to be applied in the metaphysical or mental world (Yetzirah). Society has rules and moral maps to live by, dictated by the will of minds in power, and administered to a large extent by religion. In our families these influences include pride and wisdom of the elders. These are the available resources, good or bad, right or wrong, useful or detrimental, to find mental balance, which ultimately affects our judgment.

It is difficult to understand mental balance, so abstract rules get developed. Even the halfway house cannot instill understanding of balance; they only give guidelines for living the "good life", much like religion does.

In the non-physical world the will of unknown entities can influence our balance. Consider the possibility of non-familiar entities proffering thoughts directly into your stream of consciousness or unconsciousness without you realizing that it is of an unknown source.

In the physical world we get the message of imbalance instantly. For example, we walk off a cliff or we stick a body part into boiling water. In morality and ethics, the result of mental activity (which is always off balance), is called karma.

There are many who misinterpret the good intentions of Messiahs like Buddha and Jesus, so they subsequently become more unbalanced. You must, therefore, learn the art of being stationary, non-participant, and non-imaginative (in other words, to simply observe) so as *not to misunderstand* – to stand balanced. Alternatively, you can learn to be neutral for periods of time, say during meditation, in order to allow clear vision. When in a balanced state of mind **only a slight intent will begin the proverbial ball rolling.**

Imagine that you could stand still on a platform, which is balanced on the point of a needle. Or, imagine a potter crafting the perfect vase on a spinning wheel. This requires a mind absent of foreign thoughts. For, once the imagination and dialog start up, then, the game is over and the potter will falter, and the vase will cave. If you want to influence the world around you, both your personal world as well as Universe at large, once balance is achieved, then maintained, just a little imagination will tip the scales as intended.

As an example of how the imagination will create karma, retailers depend on the psychological impact from advertising; people habitually imagine that an item would be nice to own, to decorate their world. Willy-nilly, they imagine the item inside their personal world. Imaginings are alive and will stick to your aura like glue. A person with limited self-control will have lots of these karmic images attached to them. What I have seen is when these people get extra money and time then they will make the purchases, generally wasting money because they likely had no real need for the items. We need to have increasing control over our imagining, thus controlling our lives positively and fostering improvement.

Different Types of Thoughts

In order to clearly communicate your thoughts and images, it is essential that your thinking is clear and your sensitivity is keen. It is important that you become familiar with what is going on in your mind, and to be aware of where your thoughts originate.

I hear a dialog in my head that continues to maintain my world, as only I know it to be. Since I am a Spiritual Being I am observing the personal little dialog (*ego*) of my body. But *the dialog does not necessarily originate from my consciousness*. How would I know? I used to identify with the dialog as totally mine. Now I recognize that the dialog is not mine totally, and that I have simply given a default okay to run continually. I am suspicious that another entity might be slipping into the conversation. I certainly do not want to buy into any other entity's storyline automatically; that would be like a union and guilt by association.

The ordinary person goes about their business taking care of the priorities on their list and responding to events as they come up. Plans will be made for work and family requirements. All seems to be okay and the person seems to be able to get through each day. Yet there is always a façade, even though the flow may seem to be natural and appropriate. Behind the inevitable façade, there are outdated and wrong opinions and beliefs which tend to debilitate judgments and understandings, ultimately affecting our physical world.

As a non-ordinary person, interested in finding and fixing problems and perfecting your life's path, it would behoove you to understand the inner workings of your mind behind the façade. Images coming into your mind from observations outside of your world become clouded by all sorts of aspects of your mental makeup, your mind set. These aspects include opinions, beliefs, built up clones of your parents who still talk to you from within, sadness from prior experiences, and the list goes on. Understanding your mind may take a lifetime, but progress can be made and enjoyed incrementally.

A good metaphor for our memory is that of a cave, with stalagmites and stalactites built from repeated experiences. The unconscious part of our personal mind includes the buildup of old lessons, clones in our mental landscape, trauma, and other experiences. The processes and memories now unconscious were once in the conscious foreground.

It should be mentioned that everyone's mind has elements of omnipotence and omnipresence, both consciousness and unconsciousness. Remember, your consciousness is a characteristic of Spirit as it permeates everything:

- Dialog of the little personal ego
- Spiritual EGO of the world soul
- Spiritual ideals
- Matter, space, ...

Separating and being able to distinguish types of thoughts are useful in learning any form of perception. When most people look at their own thoughts they generally do not categorize them very much or discern their origin, let alone intellectualize about their extra sensory perception.

A thought can be represented by a word or a series of words, or any combination of symbols. Our thoughts are not completely represented by the words describing them. Conversely, thoughts may be complete even though there may not be proper words to describe them. The comprehensive listener may not only hear the words but may receive the entire set of thoughts, which might include mood, feelings, and relevancy, and so on. At times a single word can cause a flooding of your consciousness with a complex image, emotions, links, and so on.

Manipulating ideas, e.g., mixing ideas together, overlaying images into consciousness, or by carefully choosing words to represent them, beckons forth changes in our world and thus changes in Universe. Your particular selection of words, thoughts and perspectives, contribute to finding your personal path.

On the molecular level, there is a communicative process performed by RNA molecules during the duplication of DNA molecules, changes in growth, functioning of hormones and reflexes, and so on. From the brain to the molecules of the entire body, there is the experience of communicative thought and thus, I believe, even cellular recognition of images.

Images

Being otherwise untrained, the ordinary person experiences a mix-up of thoughts during any particular stretch of time. Your Holy Guardian Angel always observes, however, from the highest level you are capable of understanding, down through the planes.[22] Because the mind can be stuck by cathected[23] (emotionally charged) images on a lower level, one would understandably tend to misinterpret thoughts coming from higher levels.

Images and therefor thoughts could be categorized many ways, such as follows:

- Mental, emotional, physical, mundane

- Organic images from your body (hunger, other senses)

- Your own creation (most likely from our higher self)

- Your own creation (cognitive learning)

- Creations of others (you get by telepathy)

- Incoming thoughts captured by your aura (unknown source)

---
22 The planes are seen in the Sephiroth of the Tree of Life.
23 See <u>An Elementary Textbook of Psychoanalysis</u>, by Charles Brenner, MD.

Even though an image can have been emotionally charged, they still can be modified. The energy within an image is symbolic and can be nullified, modified and barred from consciousness. As above, so below! Deal with them as if they are real; treat them with respect but deal with them by command and commitment. When they appear on the screen of your consciousness, ask yourself, Is this an image or thought cherished by me? If not then put a priority tag on it to deal with it or perhaps do something like the following:

- Overlay an image you want to dispel with a red circle and a red diagonal slash. It will cancel the symbolic meaning of the image beneath the red slash and remove cathected energy for better usage. Go ahead and see that energy being redirected toward where you want it – marry that energy quantum to the image of your choice.

- Discharge clones, which are a kind of modified image due to a buildup from repetition. Typically like the clones of your parents or friends, whose voices we can hear on occasion when triggered. Again, render the image empty by moving the energy as above.

- Tag the image with a script you state to your unconscious, such as:

"I want you to present this image to my consciousness for proper disposal at 18:00 o'clock tonight; if I am busy remind me of my commitment."

Conscious images are the essence of thoughts; thoughts are the essence of communication. Communication abounds in direct proportion to the development of the fabric at the expanding edge of Universe. Communication consists of mental activity using the meaning held in symbols. The human perception of Mind is experienced by the entire communicative system, which is in essence the entire extended body. The nervous system carries communication between and among ganglia and between and among all other cells. In addition, chemicals and hormones form another system of communication between the central nervous system and individual cell receptors. Each cell has its own internal sensual thresholds and thus experiences communication with messages in the form of images containing symbols, so be it those symbols are chemical structures.

Mindset

Include the "Beginners' Mind" of Zen in the new mind-set you are building. Rid yourself of thoughts such as anger, prejudice, grief, regret, and so forth by assuming this alternate mind-set. Do this when entering your Personal Space; then go back to your normal mind-set when exiting your Personal Space, if you must.

Thoughts that come across the screen of your mind, the workings of archetypes, memories of natural self-programming at a very early age[24] – these are the types of thoughts that can become background or unconscious, or may become blockages such as with trauma. By the way, some psychological complexes may need to be dealt with in order to release yourself from your current mindset. In some cases a psychologist or hypnotherapist[25] may help to discover, see, resolve and release such blockages or trauma.

Consider that your mind set, within your personal world, is different from all others in their personal world. The plane[26] on which you temporarily find yourself depends on the selections of thoughts you frequent. In other words, if you refine your perspective by carefully selecting thoughts, images and attitude you can rise up to a higher spiritual plane.

---

24 I recall being in a crib soon after birth. I kicked for whatever reason and my toes hit one of the styles. It hurt; my reaction was to think how I would not do that in the future.
25 During my training for transpersonal therapy I was age regressed by the instructor. He brought up a traumatic experience from my childhood and helped it to be resolved. Since then I have been remembering much more of my early years, which has allowed me to understand myself better.
26 The planes identified by Tree of Life Sephiroth, or more grossly in terms of world levels.

The Astral Hologram

My idea of the building of the cosmic fabric is by the interleaving the memory of each and every physical or mental action or change of any kind. In the depth of physical existence, at the level of Planck's Law,[27] I envision a mechanism that supports the developing fabric as a hologram. The essence of a hologram can be seen in the structure of the Tree of Life, in the sense of how in each Sephirah or sphere, there is another complete pattern of the Tree of Life.[28]

The movement of mass or even the mental counterpart – the weighted value – causes a change in the curvature of time-space. Your spiritual and astral bodies emanate energy that can be seen as an aura *(referred to as EMF or electro-magnetic field)*. When a molecule vibrates, when an impulse is sent down a meridian, when a dagger carves the sign of the pentagram, or when the name of Yahweh is intoned, energy is radiated and a magnetic field is projected. A broad process of Nature allows the continuation of the universal expansion with all of the numeric permutations and statistical variations. All are thought to be stored as a part of Akasha (Astral) holograph.

---

[27] Planck's Law predicts the smallest length in meters is about 10 to the power −35th.

[28] (See Isis Unveiled, volume I, page 177 & 178, by H. P. Blavatsky; The Secrets of Dr. Taverner, by Dion Fortune; The Black Hole War, by Leonard Susskind; and Genesis section in Chapter "One", above.)

Dividing the Whole – Meta View

What we sometimes need is a meta view of the world, or parts of it, to avoid being stuck in a narrow view of life's possibilities. It will be useful to start categorizing your thoughts – various ways of dividing the whole pie,[29] so to speak:

- Categories of thoughts: physical senses, feelings, soul yearnings, spiritual bliss
- Categories of visual images: light – dark; wave length of light
- Types of sensations
- Types of intuitions
- Types of projections
- Spirits of 360 degrees
- Action, Thoughts, Substance
- Spirit, Soul, Salt
- Center to Circumference, Circumference to Center
- Physical, Metaphysical
- Known, Knowable, Unknown, Unknowable

It would be a good idea to start a list of your various ways of "dividing the pie"[1] when you attempt to analyze things. Always try to find different ways to step out of situations at hand or rise above the scene in a spiritual-view. Your spirit, your real Being, can give direction from above, if you lift your level of consciousness so as to allow such guidance. By this I mean that your mundane thoughts can be suspended while you maintain focus on mental or spiritual concepts, for example the meaning of life.

---

29 When I say "the whole" it depends on the whole of my world.

Cardinal Directions

The Sun will rise in the East and that is your terrestrial Future; as Future passes through space it is charged with the surrounding influences, magnetic flux of the planets and star constellations, and to some extent people and culture.

Facing East a sensitive person can detect particular arriving energies. Facing West, a person can see and even experience events stored in the Sea of Memories, the Astral vault of Earth's memories.

Standing on Earth facing East the immense mass of Future comes flooding over you, causing a polarity from your left toward your right through your horizontal cross – your right side electric and your left side magnetic. The returning magnetic radiation emanates from the North and flows down toward the South over the skin of the Earth, right over your body.

Because of the rotating Earth a current moves from the South through the center of Earth; Magnetic forces surround Earth. The stability of the 90 degrees of the Cardinal directions is active on Malkuth, the lowest and grounding sphere, in the world of Assiyah. The four directions are bound by powerful spiritual energies, which can be anthropomorphized into lords of each quarter.

Some examples: *(The assignment of elements to each quarter may be different than those below, depending on the philosophy in use. For example in Thelemic[30] tradition Earth is assigned to East, Water to West, Air to North, Fire to South.)*

- You would want to meditate facing East (Air) as the sun comes up to get a glimpse of the future. What you see will depend on your mental state.
- Facing West (Water) at the end of day will allow a better view of the past and relations connected to past events.
- Face South (Fire) to honor Ra and to ask the Sun spirit for healing energy, for flexibility and expansion.
- Face North (Earth) for a communion with solidarity and contraction.

---
30 See Abrahadabra, by Rodney Opheus.

Pre-wave Broadcast

Any kind of movement creates a pre-wave of advanced warning. Think of it as radiation or magnetic flux.

Imagine a projectile moving through a soft, semi-solid substance. The impulse and friction will very likely create stress lines, which you might see as cracks. The cracks were formed just in advance of the projectile's movement forward.

A boat or missile moving through water will need to cut through the water in order to control acceleration.

A projectile makes a separation or cut through material, and just ahead of the separation there will precede a buildup of stress.

Likewise, an airplane going through the air will generate vortices, sheer stress, and shock waves preceding its moving position.

Animals can feel such advance movement, because of their keen hearing and alertness to danger.

The movements of a person over a time period create its own order of proceeding energy. A fabric will grow from the movements like the mycelium of a mushroom. A person's energetic texture is more complex than that created by the advancing projectile.

A sensitive person can learn to feel the subtleness of another person's movements and thoughts. That kind of sensitivity is the type to be felt, not so much by the 5 physical senses, but rather intuition and clairvoyance. The fabric of movement or thought energies created will tend to channel future actions and thoughts.

Intentions of future actions will create a trend for future paths. A decision which if made would cause a change in future decisions. The physical changes most people would think of as simple "action" are actually by-products of previous decisions.

Knowing this information it is possible to see a deeper meaning that will allow for another mechanism of Mind. You can make use of multiple sequences of this mechanism where one intention builds on the previous and simultaneously builds future trends.

Therefore, when Intentions are employed and action follows, it will create a "crack", so to speak, which makes it easier to traverse that same path again. This crack is like a vacuum that breathes in the nearby items of like nature.

This is the proper understanding of how to use follow-through to enhance your life and become efficient. It also tells the story of how habits are formed and how the habit can eventually get a death grip on your future.

This discussion illustrates the need for[31] secrecy, privacy and protection in a special place of contemplation and ceremony, the need to seal your work place from unwanted influence by the use of a magic circle, brilliant white sphere, impenetrable egg shape, or by another banishing ritual.[32]

A SPECIAL NOTE: This may seem paranoid to those who are not acquainted but protection is a simple concept. Normally, people are in the physical mindset even if they are intellectually oriented. I present the possibilities for Astral protection because it is important for some planning, especially if your plans are of interest to unknown entities. It is fine that you create your own mode of protection as appropriate for you.

---

31 See page 54, Zen and the Psychology of Transformation – The Supreme Doctrine, by Hubert Benoit.
32 See Cleansing and Protecting Space, Chapter Two.

Fact and Truth

Truth is the product of the analysis of facts, but it is of a separate level from facts because it is an abstraction from observation.

Facts are the certainty of a situation, of a place in space and time. The dictionary says "...truths are the facts connected to an event..."

My definition is that truths are the connections tying together facts of an event. Facts do not change; they are objectivity connections in a particular space and time. The facts however are interpreted because the observer often carries extra or alternate baggage affecting the observed facts. Truths, therefore, tend to be misleading, dependent on the particular observer. Since facts are often not scientifically measured, even their value may be uncertain, fuzzy or cloudy.

A fact can hold knowledge within it, based on the particular experience of the observer. Truth can be altered by simply willing it. Truths can only be obscured, not enhanced. There are two types of truth: your truth and the truths of others.

Faith

Faith does not necessarily refer to a religion, except in a special sense. Generically, it is belief in a future outcome or in Providence to divinely supply your rightful needs. Every concept has levels of understanding, depending on your perspective, such as world view, culture or generational time frame. To get at a deeper level, you might ask for greater knowledge about the subject (see the Chapter Four – Mystical Glossary).

Something that seems like a very bad thing, that no good is associated with it, might turn out later to be some very important solution or key to a much larger problem. There is always a pendulum factor and two sides are needed for its balance. The good may not be recognized now, but eventually someone could look back and say "Yeah, there was something good that later developed."

My mantra, "Give me that which I would want", derives from the idea that hindsight is 20:20, and that it is nearly always right. So I ask my guiding Spirit (*my Holy Guardian Angel*) to look with 'future sight', where hindsight would be viewed, and to have the Grand Mind condition my current life path with *what I need now to ensure the appropriate path in the future.*[33]

In order to have faith, you must 'know' that anything is possible and that preparations have been or will be made for that 'anything' to mature in its natural way. The formula, in fact, exists and faith is its implementation.

Example of faith:

> Suddenly I am facing a foe that I suspect intends me harm. I poise myself knowing there will be a change in the environmental conditions or situation – so I wait – knowing I will make an immediate move at the appropriate time. Knowing, the move will be exactly appropriate for my optimal survival; my passive act will be to wait to capture a moment between two periods of action of the aggressor.

Faith is also like quantum mechanics where, when a light wave is split, one half will manifest a particle; you do not know which half of the wave will manifest until you look for it – always where you look is where you will find it – otherwise only a wave will exist.

---

33 See Chapter 4 – Mystical Glossary.

Secrets

Secrets function much like physical vacuums, which are caused by changes or movements in the physical world. A secret is only a secret to others without them *knowing* there is a secret. The secret exists because there is a potential action pending and this action pending will grow in potential strength depending on the nature of that action. Over time the secret you are keeping becomes an imperative. This is like a gestation period, where during the dormancy, outside influence is minimized, just like the metaphysical protective egg shell light.

An example of the inverse would be the person who does not keep a secret, who will talk to anyone about everything without consideration. They dilute their will, waste their energy and allow sabotage to enter.

The occult aspect of a secret in many ways protects us from disaster. If you do something really awesome or something that took amazing intellect and wisdom, people may attack you because they think you are lying or they are jealous; they may try to burn you at the stake!

The bottom line is that, in general, it is better to keep your thoughts and plans to yourself unless there is a need to talk about them. First analyze what aspects of your project plans need to be discussed and with whom.

Opportunities

Taking advantage of an opportunity allows you to participate in an event. There are several ingredients:

- The event must occur
- You must be in the place and time of the event
- You must recognize your role in that event
- You must initiate and accept that role's responsibilities.

To be most effective, you need to recognize that you are merely a player in the happening. Planning and discipline only assure that you are in the proper place and time to accept the position. The concepts you have will become manifested in reality, but those concepts are affecting your future, not necessarily the opportunity.

When you do not use an opportunity it may be claimed by another or it may vanish. Opportunities are like separate entities. They are born. They may enjoy existence. They can even be abused. They die. Most opportunities eventually will be reborn. Your plans should harmonize with this natural recycling of opportunities; then, your role will be performed easily, timely and pleasantly. If you feel you are about to miss that opportunity, ease up. If it doesn't fit, don't waste your time and energy attempting to force it. Opportunities reincarnate, and when they do, if you are ready the rewards you reap are often even greater and more appropriate.

Return on Investment

You either invest your time *(which includes energy)* or you invest your money or both, giving you a chance to balance your spiritual path. Let's look at the return on your investment of your time. You don't know really how much time you have. Even if you live 120 years, the number of days and hours you can invest are limited. What are the rewards you can earn that would be worth giving up the finite hours you have left? Ask someone who has a terminal disease.

You can bet the answers will include spending time with family or communing with nature or shining your soul and spirit with understanding. You will probably not hear that they will miss working for someone else or miss getting rich. Would you consider trading the time you have left for lots of money that you will never have time to enjoy? You can make lots of money, but the more you make and save the more diminished chance you will have to get rewarding memories and real life experience.

You can be here now on a nature trail or with your family – that is real and instantly rewarding. Or, you can spend your time making money and sacrifice your time on Earth and may never get to exchange that metaphysical fat for anything it is worth in real life terms. I say this because making and saving money is a process of converting physical time to metaphysical symbolism in money; having lots of money is metaphysically the same as getting fat in person, neither of which is worth much if it isn't used in a reasonable time but is in fact great liability.

The return on your investment of time in living is generally greater than the return on your investment of your time in making and saving money simply because you give up some portion of a finite allotment for living. The more money you make with the investment of your time, the less likely that saved money (metaphysical fat) will ever become a real physical experience or character building; and therefore additional investment of your time in saving money would yield less and less real value.

Oh but for one thing. Since money is only a metaphysical construct, it can be utilized as a tool to control others, so other people can make more money for you. Look, for example, at the sweatshops in many third world nations and even in our own society, with corporations choosing to work employees beyond the normal workday and starving them of their rites to enjoy after-work personal experience.

You are part of this society and part of the controlling of others by the fact of your involvement in the metaphysical money system. We all need to remember the importance of balance; else we get involved in various shades of grey or even black magick.

Zen of Making a Choice

We normally do not think of a 'deal' as consisting of a number of assumptions. In reality, deals are complex and if we considered all their conditions it would be very difficult to bring all the elements together in a single image. What I refer to as assumptions are in fact conditions of a deal or choice where you are agreeing to things unstated!

For example:

> *"Whatever the weather may be"* is assumed, when we quickly agreed that on Monday we are to meet at the beach. *"Whatever the weather may be"* is something that may be overlooked if the prior few days happened to be all sunny. Many such assumptions are very subtle and the parties are actually unconscious of the unstated conditions!

They are essentially default judgments pending in the lawsuit over your nullity.[34] It might be wise *not* to make most choices until a complete understanding of the choice is clear. This involves waiting for fullness,[35] maintaining balance and mental health while waiting.

Coupling a visual picture with an emotion of wanting or needing, or pending karma, draws forth any number of unknown conditions in the attempt to manifest or gratify the cathected visualization. Be aware that you may be setting up the karma for your soul, not just in this lifetime – perhaps in another incarnation. Not only will your karma follow you to another incarnation but your karma may draw other souls to be incarnated with you from this lifetime.

Although the person who creatively visualizes is a principal stakeholder, other entities, including inorganic entities, may be involved. Many people go on throughout the day doing this 'wishing and wanting' whenever they see something in a magazine or storefront, without considering details and ramifications; like who else might be involved or become involved.

---

34 See Zen and the Psychology of Transformation – The Supreme Doctrine by Hubert Benoit.
35 See Stranger in a Strange Place, by Robert Heinlein.

There are many more entities than meet the eye and not all have godly intentions except their bent is to usurp higher powers. Why would an unfamiliar entity give you something like what you visualize? What would be its reward? Very simple: your emotions, which were invested at the time of your visualization. Negative entities "live" on emotions. People, in fact whole societies, are leading their lives by what they want, which are generally accompanied by emotion, rather than what they need, therefore producing fodder for stray negative energies.

I suggest that you learn to differentiate between need and want. Let the needs be first serviced. The wants would be best serviced in a natural method, i.e., items will present themselves in the natural flow of energy in the most useful and timely way when you are intuitively attuned to Nature.

I am not suggesting cutting emotions from your life. I am, however, suggesting the stoppage of the selfish, willy-nilly, automatic use of emotions. Emotions should be natural manifestations with deliberate direction. An entity that has attached itself to you will bring your likes into focus and may even speak directly to you suggesting you do something it knows you like, such as eating candy or something else such that your body would receive pleasure.

I recognize the spirit and soul within me and therefore my connection to the entire universe. Now after many years in study and practice, I realize from which part of me I speak – soul, spirit or ego. My ego will repeat messages that were incoming from my soul, spirit or physical senses, invisible master, or an inorganic entity. If we know our thoughts well and their sources, they can be classified. Then we can make choices based on intelligence, rather than driven by unknown forces.

What to Leave In, What to Take Out

Let me be very clear here because it is important to always consider "what to leave in and what to take out" of self-programming. You need to know and specifically state your limits, constraints and resources.

One requirement is that you need to know how to get back home whenever you leave home. (See next section, Pre-plan Your Return Trip.)

The point here is not to overlook full and correct restrictions and conditions, especially when planning to use Spirit, unconsciousness or your Holy Guardian Angel. The lesson is to consider all possibilities and prevent what you do not want, spelled out directly and openly in your programming.

Pre-plan Your Return Trip

It is important to pre-plan your return experience from a trip. When you are at the destination, you need something to focus on to alter your path and get back home.

If imagining creates and starts germination of a trip idea, then it is important to imagine (before you leave home) your experience of getting back home safely and on time.

There is more than one kind of trip and we need to consider them individually:

> **Bon Voyage**: Going somewhere with your physical body, like going on a date. This seems pretty obvious; you do not just have your date leave you at the party; you want to plan before you leave home how you will get back safely.
>
> **New Religion**: Going to see what they do or how they worship in a church, compared to what you are used to. Is there going to be a way to withdraw from what turned out to be a very charismatic cult? Have you set your limits of foreign mental invasion so you implement your plan B and get back home safely?

Mental Trip: This could be induced from a drug, staring at the wall, or other ways – a trip different from the two previous examples. Again, go on your trip knowing you have a solid return plan. It consists of a good look around before you leave so that you will have a location in mind when you need to return. You also need to foresee the future situation when you would draw on that memory – see yourself in your mind remembering in the future where you now stand. This is much like the programs we make for our unconsciousness.

How to Get What You Want

Your work is staged and started on the physical plane, but as the ceremony proceeds you find yourself somewhat separated from the physical. Your focus of attention will be upon images which work to guide you in presenting your monologue; you simply slip into the Astral more and more. Communication becomes more spiritual imagery and less physical talk.

Sciences of classifications, pictures, images, dreams, and prayers are all the essence of one language. It is the language of the conscious perceptions transcending the present world limits. These techniques transcend your normal conscious limitations and allow you to program your unconscious or make requests of your Holy Guardian Angel, i.e., to pass a symbolic picture up the spiritual path into the next higher world, Yetzirah.

The communication back from Spirit to your conscious is the actual experience and physical manifestation as observed by your consciousness. It is important therefore to evaluate all events, both mental and physical, as though they are the result from your preparations and communication using the images symbolic of your needs and desires. Only in this way can you take responsibility for their existence and assume the control you seek.

Know that what you see in your mind has been conceived in the womb of Nature with specific intent. When you plant the seed of conception, all that is in the mental picture is part of the formula and will define the limits of growth during gestation. If you have doubts and fears and confusion in that mental picture then those will also grow, in unique and unpredictable ways.

Your confidence will allow you only to go boldly forward; it does not do the complete job. There is a concept that should be addressed and understood because it is what allows a person to bridge the gap between desire and manifestation; it is that which allows you to **stop your internal dialog** containing all of that negative crap, which undermines natural growth. OPTIMISM or FAITH! It is indeed difficult to define and to embrace until you master the technique. But it is as real as your world. Let us try to get a good conceptual grasp of it in a practical sense.[36]

To have a practical grasp, you need to exercise faith, without which you may become the 'Devil's Advocate'. In order to exercise faith you must be in a position to use it, divorcing previous pessimistic convictions presented by your internal dialog that you will fail.

Therefore, use an "open mind" to bridge over preconceived opinions.[37] Below is a portion of a program that could be incorporated into a generalized ritual although the particular wording is for illustrating the ideas in this chapter section:

1. Close a circle around your space.

2. After meditation, chant ohm three times, Chant Yahweh three times forming a triangle on the surface of Briah.

3. I open my mind so that I bridge all prior pessimistic opinions and beliefs.

4. I raise my consciousness to a higher spiritual plane to see the truth of wants and real needs.

5. I make petition to my Holy Guardian Angel to report information back to me how to satisfy my needs.

---

36 See Faith in section State of Mind.
37 Zen, call this Beginner's Mind.

6. *I put this ceremony behind me and simply move forward knowing that there is a formula, programmed and initiated for my best interest.*

7. *State your thanks and honor your Holy Guardian Angel. Ask that you meet again soon.*

8. *Breathe deeply three times, open the circle and come back fully to Malkuth.*

Remember always that opinions do not belong resident in any part of your mind; they are for the moment or specified conditions only! Beliefs are of the same level of usefulness – the sooner you are rid of them the better you will be able to adjust to the times.

Manage your Plan of Attack

Even when an opportunity exists, there is no intrinsic reason or rationale for using it. There are millions of opportunities in this world and attempting to use them all will define you as the "wave-tossed man."[38] You will be most effective and successful if you do one thing at a time.

➢ Prior to using an opportunity align yourself with your current milestone or goal.

➢ Accept that opportunity only if it clearly aligns between where you are now and your goal.

Believe in what you do. It is easier to do something the second time. Why? Simply because we know we have been successful before and, if favorable conditions continue, another channel of success is developing – this is CONFIDENCE. The *difficulty* in finishing what you start is your *doubting* the validity of the goal or of your plan of attack.

---

38 The Ronin, by William Dale Jennings.

The following procedures can be executed and monitored to reinforce your confidence and banish your doubts:

1. Identify questions you have, problems, weaknesses or flaws; enter them in the Mystical Glossary as a Trap that needs resolve.

2. With an open mind, imagine what it would be like to have your Trap really understood. Know that this understanding will be forthcoming.

3. Be knowledgeable about your subject. Become an expert on all aspects of your current endeavor; know yourself, and your flaws and how you want to use the improvements. Learn to be enthused and dynamic by being always ready to make a positive difference. You can learn about yourself through meditation and yoga but really you just have to *want to know and ask the question or state out loud* a process statement or a glossary Trap entry or just execute the ritual for "ask and you shall receive". This is what you might state:

    a. "*I want to know more truth about myself even if it is not what I expect or would like it to be.*"

    b. "*I want to know from several perspectives so I can get an unbiased understanding of my relations with Spirit.*"

    c. "*I want to know and understand my body and mind as I am, good or bad as viewed by an impartial observer, so that improvements can be implemented to make me a better person.*"

4. Isolate the major problems blocking the accomplishment of your goals. Record this group of problems into the Glossary. Analyze and dissect each problem in order to resolve doubts and yield success.

5. Learn from each experience. Consider that each experience, no matter how insignificant, confronts you for an important lesson. Your responsibility is to accept, use and learn from all of the rewards of your endeavor.

6. Confront each negativism with an even stronger statement of positive reinforcement. Suggestions of failing will come from others; some from yourself. Watch for words like "no," "can't," "doubt" and always turn them around in a forceful manner to tip the scales back to positive.

7. Put your plan into production day by day, minute by minute.

Chapter Two – Subjects Related to Natural Mechanisms of Mind

Here I introduce a specific ritual, a version of Meditation. It includes the creation of a Personal Space,[39] a place-of-no-pity. When entering your Personal Space you need to shed or temporarily set aside your normal mindset and assume the mindset described in this and previous chapters.

Meditation, **Cleansing and Protecting Space**, and **Ask and You Shall Receive** are the mechanisms needed to fully implement the techniques mentioned in the introduction.

Mechanisms are used to setup, define a tunnel and channel from your microcosmic world to the macrocosm. From the perspective of the Tree of Life, you will be connecting spiritually to Briah where your communication will be reflected back down through the spheres of Yetzirah, being transformed on the way back to you on Malkuth (Earth) as physical or metaphysical changes to your world.

---

[39] Personal Space was introduced previously and referred to as both place-of-no-pity and Astral Space.

Meditation Ritual

Meditation is a great tool and it is never out of place. For some however, meditation has somewhat of a bad reputation among people who have listened to the 'meditation gurus', with all of their draconian rules for success. You become accomplished over time and much effort. But truth is that right now anyone can master a few simple techniques *if you relax and think not about how difficult it is but instead how important it is to be a good example to someone watching you, trying to learn*. The stupendous feats some people master need not even be known to most of us.

In that you endeavor to produce good results in your projects, meditation is always a way to improve your techniques and your results in general. Even though you may be clearing your mind during meditation, unconsciously you will be searching for a solution to your serious needs. Your unconsciousness may not be self-aware like your conscious is, but your unconsciousness is certainly committed to its own workings based on the resources available it.

Here are some meditation tips:

- ❖ **Looking at the Sky for a Quick Reset**: Whenever you find yourself unable to focus, worried, confused or the like, find a place outside, without distraction if possible, where the sky is relatively unobstructed by buildings and wires. Find a place to lie on your back or relax yourself against something. Stare straight up so as to flood your entire mind with sky. Keep looking with a gesture of abandon and you will find that your attention will be sucked upward and out of the troubles of the day and the moment. It is a perfect time to commune with the other spirits. Find out how beautiful the sky is, and how large and awesome. You may even get the idea that the sky is a reflection of your true inner self. You might find comfort. Even for only briefly you may find a meditative moment. The dialog of your physical self can be set quiet allowing your soul to soar.

- ❖ **Asana:** This is your sitting position, in which you will be comfortable, balanced, and alert. Moon smiles. *(Zen is beautiful.)*

- ❖ **Relaxation Ritual Instructions**

  - *Get into your asana position.*

  - *Close your eyes. Slowly take a deep breath, exhale; take another slow easy deep breath.*

  - *Think about how your breathing relaxes your entire body.*

  - *See that your impurities are always moving out of your body through your skin.*

  - *Feel how all your parts are working together to make this an enjoyable experience.*

  - *Each breath carries the life force of Universe right into your blood, which flows to every cell in your body.*

  - *Allow your attention to focus on your cranium muscles, move them, and let them relax, completely letting go.*

  - *Notice your eye muscles and feel them relaxing completely.*

  - *Feel all the other muscles in your head and allow them to let go and relax.*

  - *Do the same with all the muscles of your shoulders and arms and torso.*

  - *Continue to relax all the muscles down to the tips of your toes.*

- ❖ **Consecration**[40] **to Associate with the Sacred:** This is to dedicate your personal space and the articles (referred to as weapons) in your space. You will begin in the physical with your mind and focus in the place where you perform the relaxation. The dedicated space is really your astral room, place-of-no-pity or what I call Personal Space.

    If you have a physical room, paint or cover your meditation walls with the colors:

East	Yellow	the Future surmounting the horizon;
South	Red	the Sun's life giving warmth for Earth;
West	Green/Blue	the living and the sea of memories;
North	Black	the cold hard Earth.

    (You might have your own theme — that is fine. You might want to follow the Thelemic Magick system, which is nearly the same.)

    However, if you are in a temporary location, see in your mind the room with the four colored walls and ground of stone and ceiling open with a light emanating from above your head, which could be Sun or Moon.

    Whatever you do during meditation or by using a ritual from Mechanism of Mind, you should do it in this Astral Room. Only you can go to this room. Make it that way. Next, cleanse and protect this space by choosing one or more of the techniques from Cleansing and Protecting Space (see next chapter section).

---

40 Let the consecration be simple. Here is one that can be uttered aloud each time an item inside your Personal Space needs to be clean and dedicated for efficacy. "By the power vested in me by Spirit as confirmed by my existence in my world I consecrate *this item* dedicated to performing in the following ritual and ceremony."

- ❖ **Construction Specific Intent:** This technique is very effective and can be utilized to save lots of time and effort in physical building, whether it is house, machine, paper plans, writing a book, and any other construction. Go into your standard meditation space where you will not be disturbed for up to an hour. All you do in this meditation is run through the plans in as much detail as required to see in your mind each and every part and their relationships. The result is that when you go to do the work it will go fast, easy and get done right.

- ❖ **Mantra:** Many mantras are good but be sure you know its entire meaning. This can be very complex using sigils and talismans, but I generally use only two verbal mantras.
    - "Give me that which I would want."
    - "I am that, I am."[41]

Go through a relaxation technique, which will leave you in a calm state of mind, very much like a hypnotic sleep. In a way it is like separating from your physical body, which removes some physical and psychological demands. As the soul emerges separate from your body, you are propelled into the astral part of the lower formative world of Yetzirah. This will happen although you might not realize it at the time.

Your environment is ready and your body is relaxed. Just watch the thoughts go by for a while and maintain this state. If you want to stop the thoughts then make a decision to check on how a part of your body feels or some other question where you must focus. You will notice that the train of thoughts you were having has stopped temporarily. Listen carefully without participating and you may notice that what you hear as self-talk was proceeded by a smaller voice – your ego was simply repeating the small, more deeply penetrating voice and taking credit. Don't worry if you can't just turn off the dialog. If you can figuratively step back and not buy into story lines, you should be fine to proceed. While watching the thoughts it is possible to categorize and analyze them, if you wish.

---

41   See The Moses Code, by James F. Twyman.

What about extreme attitudes and your old stale beliefs and stinking opinions? Are they as easy to step out of as stopping your dialog? *These are the subjects that justify further inquiry, which might be discovered by using the Mystical Glossary.*

Meditation should be targeted for specific effects. Sitting in asana might seem as doing nothing, but your unconscious knows of your intentions and may guide your thoughts and images. You also may be guided intuitively, during your meditation, by your Holy Guardian Angel. From your Personal Space after cleansing and preparing you may access your Holy Guardian Angel, but I encourage you to wait until you have read this entire book and practiced meditation a few times. The following is an example of how to connect with your Holy Guardian Angel. It is only part of the instructions associated with a larger script.

- ❖ *Vibrate Ohm slowly, allowing the sound to reverberate or resonate in your head. Chant[42] three times to connect (ground) you rigidly to Earth.*

- ❖ *With intent to reach your Holy Guardian Angel, chant Yahweh three times. Each time pronounce it in two long syllables, Yah-weh, allowing the resonation in your head. Imagine each chant moving out from you and finally running into the sphere of Briah, which is not penetrable. The three chants will hit Briah in a triangular figure. You may find you Holy Guardian Angel facing you inside the triangle.*

- ❖ *You now have a private channel for communication. Be prepared with your anticipated conversation. Ask about your Holy Guardian Angel, like his or her name and other questions. Ask your Holy Guardian Angel to help you to learn to receive intuitive guidance and ask that he or she guide you in specific topics. Be aware that it might take you several attempts before getting a full open dialogue, but don't be negative for your Holy Guardian Angel was there; you can count on that.*

---

42 Always chant a slow, nasal resonating sound as you incant each letter, letting "One" letter merge into the next.

Cleansing and Protecting Space

Here are several ways to remove entities, snoops and influences from your space:

- **Grounding**: This consists of multiple methods. When you stand at the physical alter and prior to any rituals, make certain that your feet are planted solidly on the ground without shoes and socks. If you are in the house visualize your feet as bare and extending down into the earth by means of your body's electro-magnetic field or aura. When you address your Holy Guardian Angel, visualize Earth as the world of Assiyah. These techniques will allow the circular movement of energy when you address your HGA, your unconscious, or the Grand Mind.

- **Stand in the center facing East**. Imagine a brilliant white point in your very center, behind your solar plexus. Imagine it to grow to be a brilliant white sanitizing light. Let the light grow until it reaches out so that your walls are enclosed. The space will be clean and temporarily protected, provided as long as you hold the visual image. Allow or command this white shell to become upheld in the background while you proceed with your operations.

- **Encapsulate yourself and your aura** (with as much of your extended aura as you wish) in an egg shaped shell of brilliant white light. Inside you can expand a point of sanitizing light, as discussed above, if you wish. To maintain this shell of protection you either keep it in mind or give it the attribute of duration for a specified time or event trigger like leaving your Personal Space.

- **Perform the Lesser Banishing Ritual.**[43] This is probably not necessary for the most part. I include it here for your consideration when looking into other reading materials.

---

43 See <u>Modern Magick</u>, by Donald M. Kraig, or many other books on magic.

- ❖ **Draw, imagine or in some way craft** a closed circle around your immediate meditation space, consecrating the circle and giving it the properties you wish for protection. Open circle when entering or exiting and close it with a square knot when entering.

- ❖ **Pre-load your physical** and/or astral space with magical weapons such as altar, dagger, cross, and candles. Consecrate these items when you re-consecrate your space.

Raising Consciousness

If we both raise our conscious level toward the higher spiritual, we will both communicate on a higher level. If only one of us rises, then the message is distorted as one perspective is askew from the other. The section Meditation-Relaxation shows an example of reaching a zenith quickly by appealing to your Holy Guardian Angel.

At the highest level of consciousness, we approach a zenith, where the I's merge with all others into Unity, where clearness of perspective is without bias.[2] The rise of consciousness potentially goes up through the four worlds of the Tree of Life (Kabalah: Asiyah (Production), Yetzirah (Formative), Beriah (Creation), and Atziluth (Emanation). A human is said to be restricted in the height to which he/she is able to visit, but there are ways to get glimpses and also to have knowledge of Archetypes made practicable. Gradually becoming familiar with the spheres of the Tree of Life allows your consciousness to rise from Assiyah upward through the four worlds metaphorically. There is a limit to the height a person can elevate, depending to some degree on your soul maturity.

As far as the activities of the mind, the substance being manipulated (images in the ether) is very much like clay or plastic. The force of intention while at the zenith of your capability seems to be the drive to force the initial idea down through Creation in Briah and Formulation in Yetzirah and finally Made in Assiyah.

The point or zenith of your consciousness and awareness is the time to initiate your intention. It is the moment to cast a net, set a program, command the Mechanisms of Mind that your will be performed, give forth the visions that only you possess and held secret since your plan was set forth in **Life Organizer**. Set into motion by initiation your order for Universe to answer. This is also the kind of opportunity to set your sigils[44] into commencement. When you are in a state of heightened consciousness you might take advantage of the state of mind you are in. For the initiation of a sigil you must have planned ahead. I include the concept of sigils here for your consideration when looking into other reading materials.

Ask and You Shall Receive!

This Mechanism of Mind uses one of the prime archetypes – Reflection. It starts with the Naught's potential *(all or nothing)* to expand and contract; to spin or pulse. It is the potential of "One" to have sides and bilaterally combine with other "Ones". This Archetype also participates in responding to questions by reflecting back the question in full blooming of the answer. As the question reflected back from the world of Briah, it travels through the spheres of Yetzirah, thereby growing and maturing (gestating) with the help of the subtle energies of each sphere.

Your question should describe as much as you know and state some qualitative attributes. For example, you may ask something simple like, *"What does it mean to forgive someone who I believe hurt me?"* You might add as an attribute, *"Show me in sign or direct me to a book. Show me in such a way that no one is hurt."*

A question works much like a vacuum, in that it has missing parts, i.e., the answer to the question is the fullness of the question. For example:

> Imagine a burning question residing in the center of your chest and actually feel your solar plexus warming. Now imagine the question bursting out and being hurdled out into Universe. On the question there is missing information, links wanting of more information. When the question hits the reflective barrier

---

44 See Practical Sigil Magic, by frater U:.D:.

between Creation (Briah) and Formation (Yetzirah), it bounces back, with all those missing pieces of the question getting filled in. (*Refer to Chapter One, sections 'What to Put In and What to Take Out', and 'Zen of Choice' when writing the conditions and restrictions.*)

The concept of Ask and You Shall Receive is not new. Going back more than two thousand years, mans' faith was recorded in the honored and respected King James Bible. The number of times this concept is mentioned in the Bible seems to scream out that this is a real connection to Grand Mind of Universe and ought to be used.[45]

Quotations from the King James Bible:

John

16:24   Hitherto have ye asked nothing in my name: ask, and ye shall receive, that your joy may be full.

Ask, and Ye Shall Receive

Ye Have Not, Because Ye Ask Not

Matthew

7:7   Ask, and it shall be given you; seek, and ye shall find; knock, and it shall be opened unto you:

8   For every one that asketh receiveth; and he that seeketh findeth; and to him that knocketh it shall be opened.

9   Or what man is there of you, whom if his son ask bread, will he give him a stone?

10   Or if he ask a fish, will he give him a serpent?

---

[45] I personally testify that asking a question in a broadcast fashion to Grand Mind does in fact work.

11	If ye then, being evil, know how to give good gifts unto your children, how much more shall your Father which is in heaven give good things to them that ask him?
18:19	Again I say unto you, That if two of you shall agree on earth as touching anything that they shall ask, it shall be done for them of my Father which is in heaven.
21:22	And all things, whatsoever ye shall ask in prayer, believing, ye shall receive.

Luke

11:9	And I say unto you, Ask, and it shall be given you; seek, and ye shall find; knock, and it shall be opened unto you.
10	For every one that asketh receiveth; and he that seeketh findeth; and to him that knocketh it shall be opened.
11	If a son shall ask bread of any of you that is a father, will he give him a stone? or if he ask a fish, will he for a fish give him a serpent?
12	Or if he shall ask an egg, will he offer him a scorpion?
13	If ye then, being evil, know how to give good gifts unto your children: how much more shall your heavenly Father give the Holy Spirit to them that ask him?

John

14:13	And whatsoever ye shall ask in my name, that will I do, that the Father may be glorified in the Son.
14	If ye shall ask any thing in my name, I will do it.
15:7	If ye abide in me, and my words abide in you, ye shall ask what ye will, and it shall be done unto you.
8	Herein is my Father glorified, that ye bear much fruit; so shall ye be my disciples.

15:16   Ye have not chosen me, but I have chosen you, and ordained you, that ye should go and bring forth fruit, and that your fruit should remain: that whatsoever ye shall ask of the Father in my name, he may give it you.

16:23   And in that day ye shall ask me nothing. Verily, verily, I say unto you, Whatsoever ye shall ask the Father in my name, he will give it you.

24   Hitherto have ye asked nothing in my name: ask, and ye shall receive, that your joy may be full.

James

1:5   If any of you lack wisdom, let him ask of God, that giveth to all men liberally, and upbraideth not; and it shall be given him.

4:2   Ye lust, and have not: ye kill, and desire to have, and cannot obtain: ye fight and war, yet ye have not, because ye ask not.

By the sheer number of quotations in the Bible it appears that this is a very important concept given to mankind.

I have taken the concept one more step: *Ask the object itself.*

Have you ever lost or misplaced an object? There are two steps to take. Before you begin to search for a missing object, anthropomorphize it into a spiritual entity by simple respect for the object, and thereby honoring it and endowing it with some of your spiritual energy. It does possess a certain amount of an energetic core by its very existence and by its having been used if it is a tool. Indeed place some of your personal vitality into the object.

Be clear on just what you are doing. Remember to include specific timing constraints and limitations.[46] You will communicate with the object telepathically. In your mind see the object's image while talking directly to the image. Ask that its location appear in your consciousness or guide you directly to it.

---

46   Refer to Chapter Three, sections 'What to Put in and What to Take Out' and 'Zen of Choice', when writing the conditions and restrictions.

You may be required to either wander around mindlessly to be guided, or forget about it and go to next task while awaiting the answer – it will surely come to you when your mind is relatively free or you will be jolted to attention at an appropriate time. This is where you must do your part – that is, you must be ready and aware to grasp that opportunity, which is or which will show the answer.

Here is an abbreviated example of how to use this mechanism as a ritual in a ceremony:

1. *Mentally clear your space and mind.*

2. *Imagine the complete question appearing in your mode of display, for example as a picture or words or feeling.*

3. *Invest the image of the question with emotional energy.*

4. *Place the charged image into mid-body, behind your solar plexus.*

5. *Let the energy build until warm and expanding in your solar plexus.*

6. *When your emotion energy swells with pressure, let it burst and send this question into Universe. In your mind, see the question going out to the Grand Mind to be answered.*

7. *Forget it all and continue with your other business. When time is right you will be given the answer.*

Chapter Three – Change Management

In this chapter you will learn how to create programs and a script for their installation and tying the programs together if necessary. You will learn to channel the program and script up your spiritual conduit to the appropriate spheres of the higher world of Yetzirah.

Moving Forward

When you work on something as important as your life path, knowing that your example will repeat in future human nature because others will copy you, it is best to take a few minutes to reset your state-of-mind and balance. I recommend you meditate before and during form editing: use the Sky, relaxation or quick relaxation, sitting with open mind, mantra, or whatever it takes to calm your mind and prepare you for serious work with **Life Organizer.**

In order to seek improvement you must honestly see your flaws first, something difficult to do. Your first task, which will be your bootstrap into a better self, is to initiate the search for your flaws by using Mystical Glossary and creating an un-conscious program.[47]

The idea of flaw can be taken to another level – that of missing concepts or talents which you know about in others. Instead, for example, a person who has never experienced certain mental facilities, such as to read minds or to see auras, might consider these as weaknesses and name them as flaws of omission in his or her natural aptitude.

In order to improve yourself there must be changes made to your knowledge, maturity and understanding. You will need to identify processes that will transform your flaws or acquire new talents or even guidance and knowledge.

---
47 See Chapter Four – Mystical Glossary.

The Analysis

This section may seem like I suggest listing all of the flaws, habits, beliefs and so on that you think about yourself. Make the task easy by starting with a specific improvement you would like to make. It might be guidance or knowledge or a tick. You may list lots of items but simply pick one or two flaws to work with at a time.

- ❖ **Identify Flaws and Omissions**: List flaws such as mental, emotional or physical habits. Not that these things are bad per se, but any habit can get out of control unless continually monitored and managed. What are the environmental hurdles to your improvements and what are your beliefs and opinions that hold you back? What is it that some people have but you do not? (*I do not mean possessions*.) What is it that other people object to about you? Looking around what do you see in abundance? What about you are you showing to others that could be improved?

- ❖ **Create Processes to Fix Flaws and Omissions**: What are the processes required to morph your world (your personal environment and yourself) to overcome the flaws you listed? If you are working to learn a talent previously absent (omissions), identify or research all that is required to study and train for this inclusion. Think about what has been part of your past that keeps you stuck. What you discover may require a "filter" program; this can be an unconscious process, setup to prevent interference with your plans.

Take a good look at the following outline. It shows the structure leading to the complete ceremony, specifically designed to assist you in correcting flaws you have found.

Flaws to Ceremony Chart

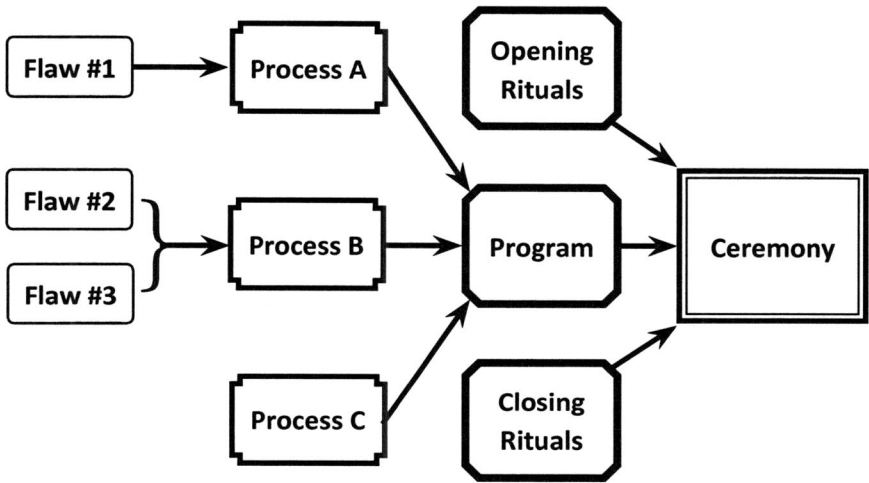

Notes:

1) There may be more than a single flaw related, such that they can be grouped together (Flaws #2 and #3).

2) A single flaw may require more than one process to be fixed (Processes B and C).

~

After the creation of the required processes, combined into the form of a program, inserted into your unconscious mind and initiated to run in the background, your entire life will be altered.[48] It is important that the processes (program) for change be well thought out since you do not want to put useless or insidious ideas into your mind.

When you create Process Statements or Glossary entries, use simple primary thinking sentences.[49] Use subject-verb-object with only required adverbs and adjectives. At the same time make certain that nothing important is left out.

---

48 See the section State of Mind for the explanation of your unconscious, also see Chapter Four – Mystical Glossary and Chapter Three – Change Management.

49 See <u>An Elementary Textbook of Psychoanalysis</u>, by Charles Brenner, MD.

If courage for you means to avoid conflict by getting someone else to fight for you but taking the credit because you got the job done, then, your concept of courage might be in need of refinement. The process statement would be the description of courage for you in the future. It might read this way:

> *"When a situation approaches with a possible conflict, **I will strengthen my courage** by my willingness to understand and be reasonable toward other points of view, but **I will stand up for what I believe is right.**"*

Your insight might lack substance and definition in the beginning. This may take several attempts. It will always be the case starting out, thus my mantra *"Give me that which I would want..." (If now I could look back from the future to now.)* Remember that self-improvement is well worth the effort!

Throughout all of your rituals, maintain the attitude that you would like to get what you would have received from 20/20 hindsight.[50] This is not only a good mantra; it is also a layer of protection.

An entire ceremony might be laid out from individual rituals, for example:

- *Meditate for relaxation*
- *Create your Personal Space*
- *Consecrate the space and walls and Brilliant Shell of Protection*
- *Chant Om three times to get in synch with vibrations of the spheres and grounded in Earth.*
- *Chant Yahweh three times, each time visualizing that you will be directing your spiritual quest up the path leading to Archetypal world of Briah, ultimately toward Yahweh, connecting with your Holy Guardian Angel in the process.*
- *Look in the triangle which was formed by your three projected Yahweh chants. Realize that the triangle formed a plane upon the impenetrable world of Briah.*

---

50 See Specific Trap 'Faith in Spirit's Meta-View' in Mystical Glossary example.

- See the face of your Holy Guardian Angel. The image may have no facial features; no need to worry; you can ask that the angel appear in any form you wish.
- State your business out loud and supplements of clear concise images as appropriate. Ask questions as they occur to you, such as your guardian's name.
- Speak your thanks and honor to your Holy Guardian Angel
- Close your Personal Space
- Fully come back to where you were prior to the ceremony.

Script Templates

Let me run through an example of requesting guidance and insight. This example does not show the use of forms due to the immediacy of the request.

- ➢ I will use my favorite mantra, which is also a command, "Give me that which I would want."
- ➢ Let's say I want to go with the flow of things as I approach a fork in the road and I happen to be on vacation. If only for my sanity I should be happy with whatever I get, but I want to take my chances with some guidance from a higher source. For the sake of safety I pull onto the side of the road.
- ➢ I face east and relax, clear my mind by watching thoughts, imagine my astral Personal Space.
- ➢ I chant Yahweh three times up my spiritual link to where the chants bounces off Briah (the Archetypal world of Reflection) forming a triangular mirror
- ➢ I see the well-known face of Joseph, my Holy Guardian Angel, and say "Grant me this command."
- ➢ I chant "Give me that which I would want! May my path be one with heart, adorned with resources, which I need to complete my trip timely and safely?"

- ➢ I state "I respect and honor you, may we reunite again."
- ➢ Then I relax.
- ➢ I start the car and continue on, knowing (having faith) that I will go the correct way. Fact is I would expect a sign to appear and show me the way that I just described.

Other examples may well go through the details using the forms, such as would be the case for creating a full tree of knowledge about quantum physics.

Now let us take a look at samples of scripts for the three techniques described in the introduction.

If you have not created your Personal Space follow the instructions about creating it in the section Meditation Ritual and the sub-section Consecration. Physical space is not required but is a good idea. Your Personal Space may seem to be in your physical area where your body is located but at the same time your mind is in the Astral. You want to be able to enter this space using your imagination at times when your physical space is unavailable. You will want to create a script for consecrating the space, sides, circle, your body, and all other items in your space at the time of your ceremony. Once you do this you can shorten these preparations to a quick procedure within your mind alone.

There are two ways to proceed with your mental participations as you sit in asana performing the ceremony only in mind:

1. You can see yourself in the personal space from a distance; or
2. You can experience yourself in the personal space such that you are immediate and active in the scene.

You may start by seeing the space from a distance but you must enter the space and create a circle from within where your Astral body is performing the ceremony. To make the switch if you are viewing from a distance, simply make the decision to be in the scene, or switch back and forth without making physical attempts.

Technique to Install a Program into Your Unconsciousness

There are two sources for the program:

- ❖ "Process Statements" field on Processes form.
- ❖ "Question" field on Traps form.

In this technique you will insert the program in your unconscious mind.

Follow instructions in section Meditation Ritual in general to prepare your body and mind.

- ➢ Enter your Personal Space.
- ➢ Cleanse and protect your Personal Space.
- ➢ Get into your sitting position.
- ➢ Close your eyes, if necessary while focusing your mind.
- ➢ Perform your breathing exercise.
- ➢ Relax your entire body (your mind must remain awake and alert).
- ➢ Stand if you wish.

1. Know that your unconsciousness is active and accessible to you by way of intent and imagery.

2. Know that your unconsciousness is multi-faceted and organized so that when you communicate a program script for it to incorporate, it will store that program in the most appropriate way for it to be effective.

3. Address your unconscious mind as you would any entity and ask it to **accept the following program and to initiate the program automatically as scripted with inclusion of specific details.**

4. Ask your unconsciousness to **make your requests private and secure just like your Personal Space was secured.**

5. State (and clearly visualize) your program to your unconscious mind as a command and, at the same time, see in your mind the outcome of your unconscious program having been executed. The visualization should be quick, clear and energetically charged.

    ➤ Sample 1:   *Wake me up tomorrow morning at 5:45.*

    ➤ Sample 2:   *Instantly wake and warn me anytime someone is attempting to enter my home or even near my home thinking about entering.*

    ➤ Sample 3:   *Review my childhood memories and, if found, alert me of memories about being treated with disrespect.*

    (You may at this point provide remedy for the transgressions of others, such as forgiveness).

6. Thank your unconsciousness for this relationship and honor your unconsciousness for being ever vigil toward your needs.

7. Open the circle in your Personal Space, from the inside.

8. Exit your space, and as you do, allow yourself to see your Personal space from a distance.

9. Allow your Personal Space in the Astral to disappear so that no one else may find it.

10. Completely drop the visualization and completely forget all thoughts of the entire ceremony. Know that your unconscious mind will perform as requested in the proper place and time.

Technique to Request Guidance from Your Holy Guardian Angel

Again, there are two sources for the program:

- ❖ "Process Statements" field on Processes form.

- ❖ "Question" field on Traps form.

In this technique you will call your Holy Guardian Angel and make your request for assistance.

You may ask your Holy Guardian Angel to answer questions, guide you down your spiritual path or insert the program you provide into the Grand Mind to be executed much the same as done in the prior technique.

1. Follow instructions in the section Meditation Ritual in general to prepare your body and mind.

    ➢ *Enter your Personal Space.*

    ➢ *Cleanse and protect your Personal Space.*

    ➢ *Get into your sitting position.*

    ➢ *Close your eyes.*

    ➢ *Perform your breathing exercise.*

    ➢ *Relaxe your entire body as you feel necessary.*

    ➢ *Stand as necessary or desired.*

    ➢ *Chant Om three times to ensure you are grounded in Malkuth and get in synch with vibrations of the spheres.*

    ➢ *Chant Yahweh three times, each time visualizing that you are directing your spiritual quest up the path leading to Creative world of Briah by way of your upper consciousness, your personal spirit.*

- Look in the triangle which was formed by your three projected Yahweh chants. Realize that the triangle formed a plane against the impenetrable world of Briah.

- See the face of your Holy Guardian Angel, a reflection of your highest spiritual potential.

2. Know that your Holy Guardian Angel is accessible and active anytime you make an attempt to commune; it works much like the unconsciousness but is representative of the world of Yetzirah and the spheres therein. This is the world of esoteric phenomena and metaphysical mechanics and alchemy. The Holy Guardian Angel is similar to the unconsciousness in the sense of listening to you by way of imagery. This communication is both objective and real and works through your creative imagination.

3. Know that every one of your actions, words, and symbolic meanings exists as part of the Akasha matrix; so that when you communicate with a spirit of the spheres of Yetzirah to respond to, know that will it have an effect upon the entire universe and specifically upon your world.

4. Ask your Holy Guardian Angel to **accept the following program, direct it to the appropriate part of Grand Mind and initiate the program as directed in the ceremony script.**

5. Ask your Holy Guardian Angel to **make your requests private and secure just like your Personal Space was secured.**

6. State your program aloud and seriously. Make sure that you incorporated all of the safeguards required for your safety and that of others. Along with your program statement or question, see in your mind precisely what you want to convey to this utterly powerful consciousness – The Grand Mind.

    - Sample 1:   *Holy Guardian Angel (use name if known), please join me in all endeavors of my life on Earth and guide me on my path so I may show a good working example to other souls on their life path.*

- ➢ Sample 2:   *Holy Guardian Angel, take the program I am about to deliver and present it to Grand Mind for execution.* (This program might be one that benefits Mankind by insisting on all conflicts between nations to be resolved diplomatically. It might call for a global attitude change and to resolve the intolerance among religions.)

7. Thank and honor your Holy Guardian Angel for this relationship for being ever vigil and responsive to your needs.

8. Open the circle in your Personal Space, from the inside.

9. Exit your Personal Space and as you do, allow yourself to see your Personal space from a distance.

10. Allow your Personal Space in the Astral to disappear so that no one else may find it and enter without your permission.

11. Completely drop the visualization and completely forget all thoughts related to that which you did. The visualization is to be quick, clear and energetically charged. Know that what you want exists and that, in the proper place and time, you will find it.

Technique to Plant a Seed in the Womb of Nature via Universal Mind

This program may result from the analysis of your flaws or needs, but more likely it will be designed to answer a question in great depth. Look at "Explanation, Statement or Question" field on Traps Form. Planting a seed is particularly appropriate because there is more than one way to answer a question. One way is to simply ask the question expecting a simple answer, like a dictionary lookup. Another question might be answered by taking your body to a place for a particular experience which is the answer. Yet another question would be answered by letting the question grow into a tree of knowledge.

In some situations you would plant the program in your unconscious mind, as done in the prior technique. In other situations you would present the program to your Holy Guardian Angel. In my example script I would like to grow a tree of knowledge in my world for my personal use but be guided by my Holy Guardian Angel, which can see the future needs better than I can at my daily spiritual height.

My quest at one time was to know more about Quantum Mechanics, to really understand with depth.

1. Follow instructions in the section Meditation Ritual in general to prepare your body and mind.

    ➢ *Enter your Personal Space.*

    ➢ *Cleanse and protect your Personal Space.*

    ➢ *Get into your sitting position.*

    ➢ *Close your eyes.*

    ➢ *Perform your breathing exercise.*

    ➢ *Relax your entire body as you feel necessary.*

    ➢ *Stand as necessary or desired.*

- Chant Om three times to ensure you are grounded in Malkuth and get in synch with vibrations of the spheres.

- Chant Yahweh three times, each time visualizing that you are directing your spiritual quest up the path leading to Creative world of Briah by way of your upper consciousness, your personal spirit.

- Look in the triangle which was formed by your three projected Yahweh chants. Realize that the triangle formed a plane against the impenetrable world of Briah.

- See the face of your Holy Guardian Angel, a reflection of your highest spiritual potential.

2. Know that your Holy Guardian Angel is accessible and active anytime you make an attempt to commune; it works much like the unconsciousness but is representative of the world of Yetzirah and the spheres therein. This is the world of esoteric phenomena and metaphysical mechanics and alchemy. The Holy Guardian Angel is similar to the unconsciousness in the sense of listening to you by way of imagery. This communication is both objective and real and works through your creative imagination.

3. Know that every one of your actions, words, and symbolic meanings exists as part of the Akasha matrix; so that when you communicate with a spirit of the spheres of Yetzirah to respond to, know that will it have an effect upon the entire universe and specifically upon your world.

4. Ask your Holy Guardian Angel to **accept the following program, direct it to the appropriate part of Grand Mind and initiate the program as directed in the ceremony script.**

5. Ask your Holy Guardian Angel to **make your requests private and secure just like your Personal Space was secured.**

6. State your program aloud and seriously. Make sure that you incorporated all of the safeguards required for your safety and

that of others. Along with your program statement or question, see in your mind precisely what you want to convey to this utterly powerful consciousness – The Grand Mind.

> Sample 1: *I beseech you, my Holy Guardian Angel, to assist Grand Mind in gathering and presenting information in the form of a Tree of Knowledge in any way compatible with my overall life path of enrichment to my soul.*
>
> *The tree to grow is the Tree of Knowledge of Quantum Mechanics, to include all that is known now and later including how other theories are affected. Plant the program in Grand Mind for nurturing. Let this concept form the seed, which will germinate and grow to fruition.*
>
> [You may at this point provide caveats for manifestation of the tree into your consciousness.]

7. Thank and honor your Holy Guardian Angel for this relationship for being ever vigil and responsive to your needs.

8. Open the circle in your Personal Space, from the inside.

9. Exit your Personal Space and as you do, allow yourself to see your Personal space from a distance.

10. Allow your Personal Space in the Astral to disappear so that no one else may find it and enter without your permission.

11. Completely drop the visualization and completely forget all thoughts related to that which you did. The visualization is to be quick, clear and energetically charged. Know that what you want exists and that, in the proper place and time, you will find it.

Identify Flaws

Flaws Instructions
The basic premise is that you need to make improvement in yourself so as to show a better example, thus the world is a better place for mankind. So you start by selecting a weakness or a missing skill or talent.
Since there is a significant amount of thought required of this self-improvement project it would behoove you to have a plan. Is your objective professional, personal, related to religious thought, for guidance, social, college?
Enter needed skills, missing understanding, chronic problem, mental technique desired, to name a few. Be candid with yourself, even if they are descriptions of anger, depression, feeling sad. If they are real for you, they ought to be considered.

Example – Flaws Form

Flaw Name	Problems in Environment & Resources; Faults with Self; Omissions of Talent	Detailed Description and Ideas on How to Resolve Problems, Faults or Omissions
Mind Reading	I often forget to be aware of other people's true being by watching their facial expression closely. Time moves quickly and I miss things.	Enhance Mental Facilities to include mind reading. When I still my mind and just observe, then I can see the thoughts of others, especially if they were just asked a question or they are continuing along a line of thought.
Bad Habits	Others really are bad drivers. I feel I judge others by wrongful attitudes. I am not being charitable.	Cease Bad Habits like blaming others while driving.
Control Opinions	I have dropped most Opinions; Rarely do they reappear; Sometimes new "ones" develop.	Control and exorcise old opinions. Probably need to set a program to clean out old opinions periodically, using specific parameters.
Control Beliefs	I have dropped most Beliefs; Rarely do they reappear; Sometimes new "ones" develop.	Control or exorcise beliefs. Probably need to set a program to clean out old beliefs periodically, using specific parameters.
Initial Impressions	This is kind of like my not focusing on the other's being or expressions. I go too fast or over analyze, causing me to go too slow.	Enhance my initial impressions of people. My mind races and I cannot fairly judge the environment and objects around me, so I forget names and even the occasion.

Set Processes

Process Instructions – *Phoenix Rising From the Ashes!*

The purpose of the weakness or Flaws form is to get together all the difficulties of your thinking and to gain perspective of what you have to deal with day by day. This will help to create a bird's-eye view of your overall condition and problems associated with acquisition of improvements.

Processes are all about instructing your unconsciousness, Holy Guardian Angel or Grand Mind to execute a set of process statements (program) in the background. The program is a human language statement that you compose, where you specify in detail what internal effect (personality, habitual, beliefs, psychology) you want produced.

You could set your program to make effects external to your world but that is not what we are doing in this book, except for guidance on your life path. Be reasonable with the changes; focus on converting flaws which affect you the most. You should craft processes that remove the negative parts of your flaws in such a way that you reach your Goal of showing a better example.

Identify "how" you will accomplish each improvement as a series of one or more processes. Each program may require several processes, but you need list only those most significant.

Craft an elementary process so that each action and object of that action can be easily derived. This statement should clearly describe how the improvement will be accomplished. List the action (verb) concerning each process. List the object (noun) concerning each action to help crystallize the outcome of the process.

Life Organizer is designed to help you make alchemical changes in your ability to learn, remember, enhance your intuition, going with the natural flow, and so on.
Some flaws might be combined to form a strong and binding process and thus a strong and binding result.

You can create a general process to be continued indefinitely; you will need set up a cycle and define the natural triggers or natural standards to follow.
Otherwise, you can setup a trigger which will initiate the process once or more times. Be careful, without specifying limits you could have a potentially dangerous runaway process.

When you are certain you have it right then you can set it into action (follow directions in Chapter Three, Change Management).

Maintaining a meta view of yourself and your environment will help your balance and help you to ask appropriate questions rather than having a half-baked opinion.
Try to discern needs from wants, because you might find that needs are being neglected and unconsciously making you unhappy, angry and regretful.

Looking at the example Flaws Form

The following two flaws will be combined as a single program:

Mind Reading – Enhance Mental Facilities to include mind reading.
I often forget to be aware of the other person's being or forget to look at their facial expression closely. Time moves quickly and I miss things. When I still my mind and just observe then I can see the thoughts of others, especially If they were just asked a question or they are continuing along a line of thought.

Initial Impressions – Enhance my initial impressions of people.
This is kind of like my not catching the other's being or expressions. I to go too fast or over analyze and go too slow. My mind races and I cannot fairly judge the environment and objects around me, so I forget names and even the occasion.

Looking at the **Flaw Mind Reading**, it seems that I need stillness of mind
and mind of an observer of thoughts, since I can read minds under these conditions.

Looking at the **Flaw Initial Impressions**, it seems that I need the same two qualities working to catch a first impression and a special quality of analyzing that fresh and crisp impression.

Example – Processes Form

Fault Name	Process Name	Action	Object of Action	Process Statement
Mind Reading	Awareness	Draw Back	From Surrounding	When I am faced with an interaction with any and all other persons my consciousness immediately will rise to gain higher meta-awareness, my mind will clear and the Inner dialog will cease. I will view the person's facial expression and observe their thoughts as they enter my mind. This is now my normal greeting.
Initial Impressions	Impression	Stop World	To See People	Some place on the approach of my meeting with someone, there will be a moment when the world stops for an instant; when this happens or when I make the world stop, I get a true impression of that person and the situation.

Chapter Four – Mystical Glossary

I recommend using this section any time you have a question or if you would like to define a concept or belief or rid yourself of a stale opinion. You may have found while working the Flaws or Processes forms that there were some barriers or hurdles. In most cases the dictionary is the best way toward clarification. However, sometimes you may have peculiar understandings of the meanings of ideas, words, phrases, concepts and symbols that are beyond your grasp.

If there is a question then there is also an answer. The answer lies in the true essence of the words comprising the question. I find that usually when I keep restating the question, each time being sure how I relate with each term and jargon, then the proper question will finally be asked which will calls forth, even defines, the answer.

Identify words, phrases, statements, or questions which have special meanings, lack of meanings or confused meanings, referred to as "Specific Traps".

Identify categories for the Specific Traps. Categories are referred to as "Generic Traps". A few categories are listed below for examples:

Some Generic Trap Names

- Habits I will use
- Habits I am losing
- Habits I am gaining
- Thoughts I will no longer have because I regret them
- Things I have done and regret
- Feelings of remorse
- Gaps of understanding (Questions)
- Questions I don't want asked
- High value rewards
- 1 to 3 dimensional symbols
- Things that make me sad
- Doubts
- Beliefs
- Opinions
- Foods I don't like
- People I don't like
- Past accomplishments
- Obstacles preventing success

If you have difficulty getting started, then turn to the Mystical Glossary and make your first entry, something like this:

Example #1 – Traps Form

Generic Trap Category	Specific Name / Phrase	Explanation, Statement or Question (Remember that these items will be connected to the Grand Mind for elucidation, which will be assimilated into your information warehouse.)
Habits I Want	Get Started Organizing	"When I think of my flaws or skill omissions, no matter what time of day, I will update the Flaws Form until satisfied with the final composition."
Advanced Studies	Order of Knowledge	What are the most important ideas I need to study, and what is the order they need to be studied?

Craft a statement to give a precise definition to the Trap, Get Started Organizing. The entry is called a Trap because wrong understandings tend over time to get rooted so you become locked into habitual patterns that are not so easy to shake once you buy into their storyline.

I call this glossary mystical because of the fact that you make entries with expectation for Grand Mind to illuminate your understanding of those entries. This expectation and honoring of the Grand Mind makes the connection. So it is not required that all of your questions be taken to your Holy Guardian Angel. If you want special consideration, like the sophistication of a Tree of Knowledge, it is a good idea to present it to Grand Mind using a ceremony involving your Holy Guardian Angel (see section Script Templates).

Initiate a trap process without the use of Holy Guardian Angel: You may have set up a question so that it needs a trigger to activate Grand Mind to perform on your question or request.

1. Internally or using your normal out loud voice ask your unconscious mind to support your current effort.

2. If there is no resistance then visualize the occurrence of the request being presented to Grand Mind.

3. Honor and praise your unconscious mind for its agreement to support you; then,

4. In your imagination, see the Trap, **Order of Knowledge,** waiting to be answered.

You can learn for yourself about various applications of Flaws Processes and Mystical Glossary Questions. When initiated, entries you place into the Mystical Glossary will become instruction to your unconscious mind or to (the reflexive)[51] Universe, both of which are accessible.

It should be kept in mind that all actions, physical and mental, affect Universe and are stored in the Akasha Records (Astral holograph if you will).[52] Every detail is important, like don Juan Matus says (paraphrased) "Everything you do becomes equally important in the face of your last act on Earth. Death levels the playing field."[53] The point being that no one knows exactly when they will die so every act might be your last act on Earth. So you should make every act count.

I would encourage you to get through this book even if you don't fully comprehend it at once. If the concepts are not familiar to you then I encourage re-reading several times. The exercises are not time consuming once you get familiar with the processes.

---

51 Reflexive concept comes from <u>The Reflexive Universe</u>, by Arthor Young and from my use of the Archetypal spirit seen in Briah that polarizes and reflects Ones produced in the world of Atziluth, sphere of Kether.
52 See The World as a Hologram, <u>The Black Hole War</u> by Leonard Susskind
53 See writings of Carlos Castaneda.

About Reading a Dictionary

This section pertains to the Glossary.

We often develop stigmas about words. Considering the meaning of a word through as many perspectives as possible will ensure objectivity – not only toward that word, but also toward every part of the reality of that word.

Read each definition of the words you look up. Try to find a commonality among the definitions; no matter how apparently unrelated they first appear.

Read definitions of nearby, related words to understand how a single root meaning has been generalized or varied into neighboring words.

Upon understanding the composite word as well as possible, dissect the word into syllables. Look up each syllable, individually, to see if there is a separate listing for that syllable.

Most importantly in your study, discern the single antonym most opposite in meaning to the original word.

Take your understanding to a new level and learn the numerical meaning of the letters. You can do this by researching numerology. Do not start with Gematria. Start simple. Find a simple book on numerology for the English language.[54]

---

[54] I have limited suggestions. One is <u>The Science of Numerology – What Numbers Mean to You</u>, by Walter Gibson, 1927.

Traps Instructions

Keep your Mystical Glossary up to date. When you think of another item, enter it and complete your work. When you better understand an entry, make the correction.

This training method is intended to teach you to better see the things that particularly affect your objectivity and, in some cases, prevent your total success.

Getting these things on paper is like sweeping dust out of the corners of your mind. You will see the truth in yourself and know better your relationship with your past and thereby avoid repetition of errors in the future.

NOTE: A belief is a conscious pattern. Beliefs uphold themselves with little effort because they reinforce themselves each time they execute. For this reason, I call them habits. A belief can be malignant if not restricted to particular purpose.

It is important that you maintain this awareness in order to keep abreast of changing times and lost purposes. You would logically void such a belief by writing a habit statement that is a reverse of the belief being canceled. This reverse belief would be brought to mind instead of the obsolescent belief pattern.

Enter the specific Trap word, phrase, or symbol on a line and write about it. Look in a dictionary, encyclopedia or other reference to be certain your meanings and usages are correct. Study and learn.

Example #2 – Traps Form

Generic Trap Category	Specific Trap Name / Phrase (Ritual)	Trap Clarification Explanation or Question (Use the Ask and You Shall Receive Ritual)
Habits I want Insight #1	Knowing my weaknesses	What are my basic weaknesses? Initiate the answering of this question from the center of my being, around my solar plexus or heart chakra.
Self-Image Insight #2	Be more specific	I would like to gain better utilization of my time through proper discipline of my thinking, acting. Approach each Question, Statement, Object, Sign slowly with care – as each is Vitally Important.
Mantra for Meditation Insight #3	Faith in Spirit's Meta-View	"Give me that which I would want…" if I could have future 20/20 hindsight from the future what would I want now? It is unknown now but you can ask your higher spirit, which does have that insight… thus give me that hindsight now. See Faith in Chapter One – State of Mind.
Insight #4	Foresee opportunity	"I want to have clairvoyance specific to future events *in such a way* that I easily control this aptitude as to When and what I view."
Definitions	Cathexed or cathected	Emotional psychic energy invested In an image (see Zen…, by Hubert Benoit)
Self-Image	Be more specific	I would like to gain better utilization of my time through proper discipline of my thinking, acting, Approach each Question, Statement, Object, Sign slowly with care – as each is Vitally Important.
Cool Phrases	Stupid Going to Seed	
Cool Phrases	Intelligence Containment	
Cool Phrases	Quality Circle Jerk	
Definitions	Spirit	Undifferentiated Consciousness resulting from Self-Realization: I am
Definitions	Soul	The surviving set or transcendental understandings which I call my soul, which I Expect to reincarnate and grow.
Definitions	Personality	Expression of the spirit along with ego influences based on experiences of this Lifetime.
Definitions	Ceremony	
Definitions	Ritual	
Mystical Ritual	I am That I am	The Moses Code explains this ritual (see Bibliography).
Mystical Ritual	Consecrate	Clean, honor, respect the article, dedicate the item to a specific sacred purpose.

Bibliography

Manuscript	Author	Notes, Quotes, Significance
A Kabbalistic Universe	Z'ev ben Shimon Halevi	
A Separate Reality	Carlos Castaneda	
An Elementary Textbook of Psychoanalysis	Charles Brenner, MD	
Biofeedback, third edition	M. Schwartz and F. Amdrasik	
Finding True Magic	Jack Elais	Reference skanda
Isis Unveiled	H. P. Blavatsky	Volume I, page 177 & 178
Jorney to Ixtlan	Carlos Castanada	
Magical Passes	Carlos Castaneda	
Modern Magick	Donald M. Kraig	
Practical Sigil Magic	frater U:.D:	
Sea Preistess	Dion Fortune	
Sefer Yetzirah	Aryeh Kaplan	
Stranger in a Strange Place	Robert Heinlein	
Tensegrity	Carlos Castaneda	Carlos presents a way to gather up unused and mis-located energies and apply that energy to particular places on your body in need. The concept of Intent is demonstrated.
The Black Hole War	Leonard Susskind	
The Geometry of Meaning	Aurthur M. Young	
The Moses Code	James F. Twyman	
The Mystical Qabalah	Dion Fortune	
The Reflexive Universe, Evolution of Consciousness	Aurthur M. Young	
The Secrets of Dr. Taverner	Dion Fortune	A novel with an example of Dr. Taverner accessing the Akasha Records on page 25 through 27.
Zen and the Psychology of Transformation – The Supreme Doctrine	Hubert Benoit	

Appendix A – Metaphysical Notes

Below is a chart of my notes regarding metaphysical worlds.

Joel's Categories	Level	Notes
The Unknowable (Pre-primordial)	Source of all Universal Node Universal Spore Sea of Naught Potential of "One" with potential of Polarity	We can't imagine an all containing container; nor a sea of Naught, points without dimensions. We can only do the math on what exists.
The Unknowable (Primordial)	World of Emanations – Atziluth Self-Awareness "One" Spirit Ether Sea of "Ones" Realization of Potential of polarity Universal workings beyond human Concepts	Accumulation of All Self Realization created from source Spirit transcends all levels Downward but we can detect with our normal awareness only fleeting Fragments of Spirit's Face
The Partially Knowable	World of Creation – Briah Archetype of Two Other Archetype potentials (Supra) Meta-Consciousness Spiritual laws Spiritual body – I am that I am	Archetype of Reflection uses Polarity to manifest the mirror effect Partially knowable because we can see the effect of Archetype everywhere Meta view accessible via mechanisms of Mind rituals Mental – you might think you have an original idea that could be patented and then find out someone else had already received the patent. This kind of occurrence is because in the mental plane we deal with concepts, most having existed for eons, even if it only recently manifested into your world.
The unknown but Knowable	World of Formation– Yetzirah Additional Archetypes Angels Plane – Three (Sub) Unconsciousness Forgotten memories Akasha Holographic Astral Body Symbols	3x4 = Zodiac World of Souls World of Concepts Mental & Astral & emotional Movement directed for survival
The Known	Kingdom – Assiyah Solid – Four Consciousness Physical body I am ID, Ego, Super Ego	Manifest world My personal world Look to East for Future Look to West for Past Manifest experience Cardinal directions All Possibilities All Permutations

Development from Naught:

- Within Naught there is Self-awareness potential.

- First Reflection against the Sea of Nothing: Potential of existence.

- Imperfection of the reflected self-image, in turn, produces potentials of imperfection and polarity, to be inherited in the world of Yetzirah. Polarity affects the way the "Ones" accumulate to produce all the possibilities in the expanding Universe.

- Development requires initiation by either an outside force (as in a node) or a cyclic motion inside the Naught as a potential.

- "One" is Consciousness of the Potential: "Spirit of God was hovering over the Face of the Waters".

- Two is the Scope of Development: Yin – Yang; Reflection; walking displays the Archetype of Reflection in action – left, right...left, right, and so on.

- Three is the Eclipse of Self Recognition: Trinity Symbols, of the Child; triangle rigidity; divisive as the edge of a sharp tool; Three points form the edge of action, dividing substance.

- Four points formulate solid; the physical World (Assiyah); four cardinal directions.

- Action of 3 factors substance of 4 to yield the 12 houses of the zodiac.

- Conversely, 3 splits the zodiac into 4ths, producing right angles, the elements.

Appendix B – Tree of Life Symbol

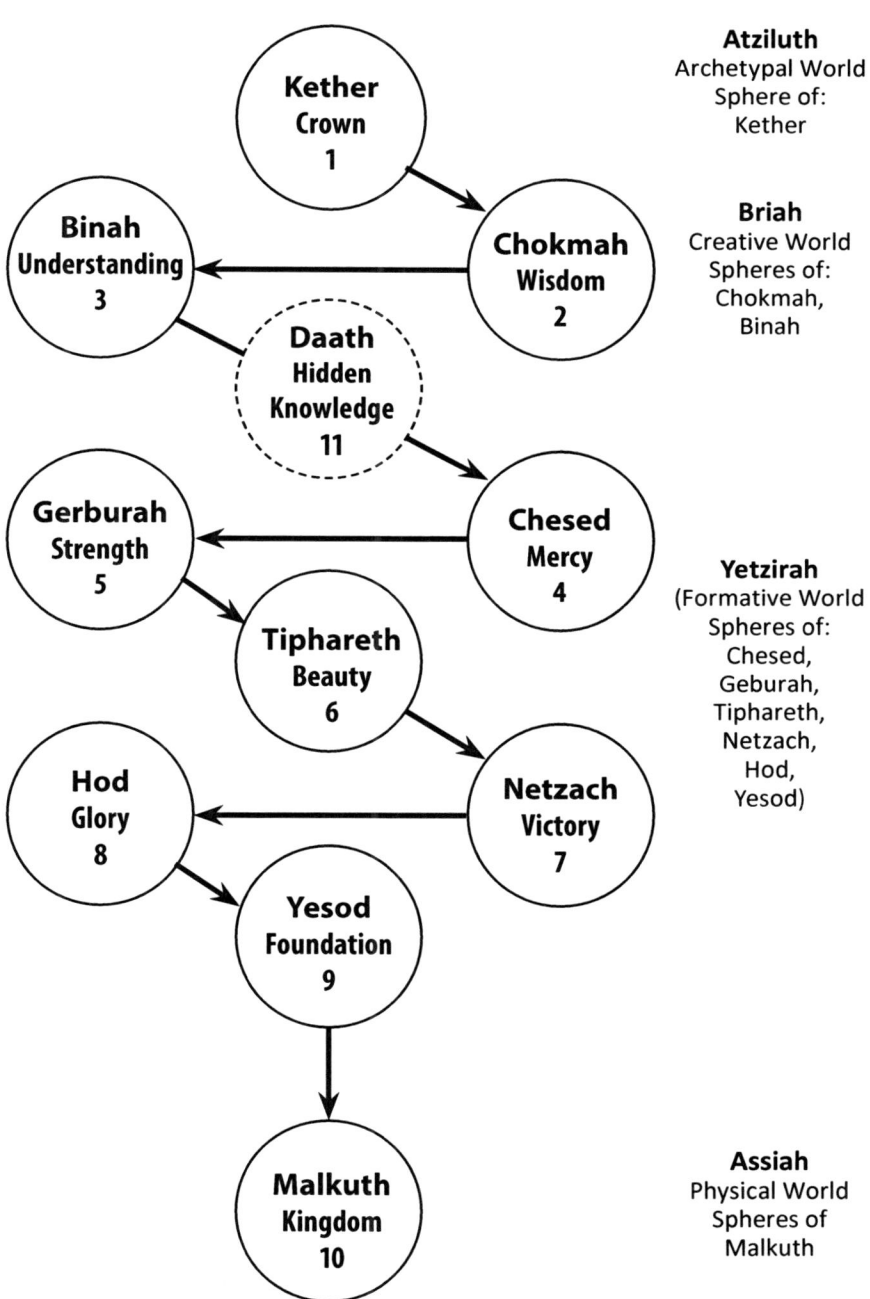

Appendix C – Forms

You are allowed to copy the following forms:

Flaws Form

Flaw Name	Problems in Environment & Resources Faults with Self Omissions of Talent	Detailed Description and Ideas on How to Resolve Problems, Faults or Omissions

Processes Form

Fault Name	Process Name	Action	Object of Action	Process Statement

Traps Form

Generic Trap Category	Specific Name / Phrase	Explanation, Statement or Question (Remember that these items will be connected to the Grand Mind for elucidation, which will be assimilated into your information warehouse.)

About Author

Joel Brown spent 4 years attending Washington State University and Western State University studying sciences, mathematics, information management, and philosophy. He studied occult and mystical teachings beginning about 1975 to present. He worked as an analyst and computer programmer from 1971 to 2004. In 2012 he became a student of natural and bioenergetics medicine.

This Yin-Yang symbol is the author's personal logo, the double star representing the 5 elements and the spiritual reflection in the duality of Universe.

Joel B. Brown, 1995

Alone

Alone within my mind I am, though many come around.
Communication's all that lives — when objects change their flight.
Some things, that is, collide with me however close they get.
Attractive fires are lit in me according to their might.
The Pen writes many letters out, but after many, many fires.
Some tiny sparks cause might blazes from impacts hardly felt.

Alone within my mind I am, though others feel the light.
Communication's all that lives — when change is warmth and light.
Some things, that is, exchange with me however close they get.
Attractive fires are lit in us according to the might.
The Pen makes many fires bright, but lets many, many die.
Some tiny sparks cause might blazes from impacts hardly felt.

Alone within my mind I am, now very few come 'round.
Communication's all that lives — and you're in life, my love.
Few things, that is, collide with me, which cause a lasting fire.
Attractive fires are lit in me, but mostly long since lost.
The Pen strokes many letters bright, but warmth is seldom had.
Some tiny sparks cause might blazes from impacts hardly felt.

Alone within my mind I am, while I too, move about.
Communication's all that lives — and some is now with me.
Some change, that is, is felt by me however close you get.
Attractive fires are seldom lit, since all but you is night.
The Pen for many hearts strikes fires, but only one for me.
Some tiny sparks cause might blazes from impacts hardly felt.

Alone within my mind you are, though seldom we are near.
Communication's all that lives — and you're my only dream.
Some dreams, that is, are warmth and light however dark it gets.
Attraction grows within my heart in accordance to my fight.
The Pen for many words of love, but my only love is you.
Some tiny sparks cause might blazes from impacts hardly felt.

Joel B. Brown, 1966